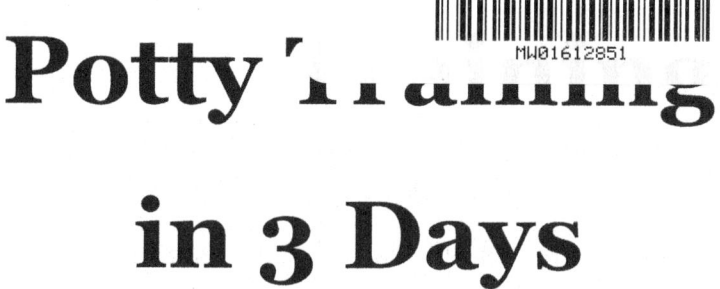

Potty Training

in 3 Days

The Practical Guide that Will Help Your Baby
to Leave the Diaper and Use the Potty.
Complete with Tips and Tricks for the Most
Challenging Kids

(For Little Boys and Girls)

by

Elena Gregory

Disclaimer Notice

Please note the information contained in this document is for educational and entertainment purposes only. All effort has been executed to present accurate, up-to-date, and reliable, complete information. No warranties of any kind are declared or implied. Readers acknowledge that the author is not engaging in the rendering of legal, financial, medical, or professional advice. The content in this book has been derived from various sources. Please consult a licensed professional before attempting any techniques outlined in this book.

By reading this document, the reader agrees that under no circumstances is the author responsible for any losses, direct or indirect, which are incurred as a result of the use of the information contained in this document, including, but not limited to, — errors, omissions, or inaccuracies.

Table of Contents

Introduction   **8**

Understanding the Child's Developmental Milestones   **11**

Positive Parenting Tips   12

Healthy Bodies for your Kids   14

The Proper Height and Weight for your Children   16

Happiness in Powerful   19

Getting Started with Potty Training   **25**

Child-Centered Training   25

Advocating For Diaper-Less Babies   25

When to Start Potty Training Your Child   26

Why it's Important to Potty Train Early   27

Debunking the Myths and Misconceptions of Potty Training   29

The ABC of Potty Training   31

Knowing If Your Child is prepared   32

Potty Training Checklist   34

Steps and Rules for the Potty Training   **36**

Assess Your Child's Readiness For Potty Training   36

Make Potty-Training Preparations   36

Be Consistent In Your Approach to Potty Training   39

Demonstrate How It's Done   41

Persevere With the Potty If He's Ready   43

Cope Calmly with Potty Training Accidents   46

The Basics of Potty Training   **49**

Potty Training for Boys   49

Potty Training for Girls   55

When To Banish Nappies   62

Weeing, Pooping and Preventing Infection   64

Making Potty Training Fun   65

When Will Nights Be Dry Too?   66

Signs that a Toddler is Already Potty-Trained   68

Potty Training in the Dark   69

Reinforcing Success   **74**

Taking Control   76

Potty-Training Techniques   87

Babysitting and Traveling   92

Tips to Assist You as the Caregiver and the Child Throughout the Experience   96

Dealing with Accidents   97

Potty Training Your Child in 3 Days   107

A Few Days Before   107

The Night Before   108

Day 1   113

Day 2   115

Day 3   116

Asking for Help from Healthcare Professionals   119

Preventing Potty Training Regression   120

**Potty-Related Problems and Dealing with
Them   126**

Backsliding and Regressing   126

Slow Progress   128

Introducing Other Caregivers   132

Being Busy   133

Fending Off Night-Monsters   134

Dealing with a Headstrong Kid   134

Training a Toddler with Disabilities   136

Tips and Tricks for Potty Training   139

Other Practical Potty-Training Tips: 152

Common Potty Mistakes to Avoid   **154**

Conclusion   **169**

Introduction

I want to thank you for downloading this book, "*Potty Training in 3 Days*".

Parents play a crucial role in potty training. Parents got to provide their children with direction, motivation, and reinforcement. They have to line aside time for and have patience with the restroom training process. Parents can encourage their children to be independent and permit their children to master each step at their own pace.

Potty training might sound sort of a daunting task, but if your child is ready, there's not much to stress about.

"Life goes on, and at some point, your child will just roll in the hay," says Lisa Asta, M.D., a clinical professor of pediatrics at the University of California, San Francisco, and spokesperson for the American Academy of Pediatrics. "When kids want to travel on the potty, they're going to continue the potty.

Sometimes that happens at 18 months, sometimes it doesn't occur until on the brink of age 4, but no healthy child will enter kindergarten in diapers." So, don't stress—your child will ultimately get on the potty and do his thing, but you'll help guide the method along. If you're able to make diapers a thing of the past in your house, experts recommend following these seven easy steps.

Your child will show cues that he or she is developmentally ready. Signs of readiness include the following:

- Your child can imitate your behavior.
- Your child begins to place things where they belong.
- Your child can demonstrate independence by saying, "no."
- Your child can express interest in potty training (e.g., following you to the bathroom).
- Your child can walk and is prepared to take a seat down.
- Your child can indicate first when he's "going" (urinating or defecating) then when he must "go."
- Your child is in a position to tug clothes up and down (on and off).

Each child has his or her sort of behavior, which is named temperament.

In planning your approach to bathroom training, it's essential to think about your child's temperament.

- Consider your child's moods and, therefore, the time of day your child is most approachable.
- Plan your approach supported when your child is most cooperative.
- If your child is usually shy and withdrawn, he or she may have additional support and encouragement.
- Work together with your child's span.

Plan for distractions that will keep him or her comfortable on the potty seat. This and a lot more on how to get your kid on the potty will be explained in this book.

Understanding the Child's Developmental Milestones

Skills like taking a primary step, smiling for the primary time, and waving "bye-bye" are called developmental milestones. Developmental milestones are things most youngsters can treat at a particular age. Children reach milestones in how they play, learn, speak, behave, and move (like crawling, walking, or jumping).

During the second year, toddlers are traveling more and are conscious of themselves and their surroundings. Their desire to explore new objects and other people is also increasing. During this stage, toddlers will show greater independence, point out defiant behavior, recognize themselves in pictures or a mirror, and imitate others' behavior, especially adults and older children. Toddlers also should be ready to remember the names of familiar people and objects, make simple phrases and sentences, and follow simple instructions and directions.

Positive Parenting Tips

The following are a number of the items you, as a parent, can do to assist your toddler during this time:

Mother reading to a toddler

- Read to your toddler daily.
- Ask her to seek out objects for you or name body parts and items.
- Play matching games together with your toddler, like shape sorting and straightforward puzzles.
- Encourage him to explore and check out new things.
- Help to develop your toddler's language by talking together with her and adding to words she starts. for instance, if your toddler says, "baba," you'll respond, "Yes, you're right—it is a bottle."
- Please encourage your child's growing independence by letting him help with dressing himself and feeding himself.
- Respond to wanted behaviors entirely; you punish unwanted behaviors (use only very brief

time outs). Always tell or show your child what she should do instead.

- Encourage your toddler's curiosity and skill to acknowledge everyday objects by taking field trips together to the park or happening a bus ride.

Child Safety First

Because your child is traveling more, he will encounter more dangers also. Dangerous situations can happen quickly, so keep an in-depth eye on your child. Here are a couple of tips to assist your growing toddler safe:

- Please do NOT leave your toddler near or around water (for example, bathtubs, pools, ponds, lakes, whirlpools, or the ocean) without someone watching her. Fence off backyard pools. Drowning is the leading explanation for injury and death among this age bracket.
- Block off stairs with a little gate or fence, lock doors to dangerous places like the garage or basement.
- Ensure that your house is toddler-proof by placing plug covers on all unused electrical outlets.

- Keep kitchen appliances, irons, and heaters out of reach of your toddler. Turn pot handles toward the rear of the stove.
- Keep sharp objects like scissors, knives, and pens in a safe place.
- Lock up medicines, household cleaners, and poisons.
- Do NOT leave your toddler alone in any vehicle (that means a car, truck, or van) even for a couple of moments.
- Store any guns in a safe place out of his reach.

Keep your child's seat rear-facing as long as possible. Consistent with the National Highway Traffic Safety Administration, it is the best way to keep her safe. Your child should remain in a rear-facing seat until she reaches the highest height or weight limit allowed by the car seat's manufacturer. Once your child outgrows the rear-facing seat, she is prepared to travel in a forward-facing seat with a harness.

Healthy Bodies for your Kids

Give your child water and plain milk rather than sugary drinks. After the preceding year, when your nursing toddler eats more and different solid foods, breast milk remains a perfect addition to his diet.

Your toddler might become a picky and erratic eater. Toddlers need less food because they do not grow as fast. It is best not to battle with him over this. Offer a variety of healthy foods and let him choose what she wants. Keep trying new foods; it'd take time for him to find out to love them.

Limit screen time and develop a media use plan for your family. External icon for youngsters younger than 18 months aged, the AAP recommends that it is best if toddlers do not use any screen media aside from video chatting.

Your toddler will seem to be moving continually- running, kicking, climbing, or jumping. Let him be active— he's developing his coordination and becoming strong.

Make sure your child gets the recommended amount of sleep each night: For toddlers 1-2 years, 11-14 hours per 24 hours (including naps)

The Proper Height and Weight for your Children

Baby growth charts for boys and girls are crucial tool health providers use when comparing your child's growth to other kids her age. Except for the typical parent, they will be somehow confused to decipher.

To make it easier for you to urge informed, we experts had a breakdown of the knowledge you want to understand about your child's physical development. Here's an easy way to check out average height and weight growth at every age:

Baby Height and Weight Growth

- **Birth to 4 Days Old**

The average newborn is nineteen .5 inches long and weighs 7.25 pounds. Boys have a head circumference of about 13.5 inches, and girls measure in at 13.3 inches, consistent with the National Center for Health Statistics.

A baby drops 5 to 10 percent of his total weight in his first few days of life due to the fluid he loses through urine and stool, says Parents advisor Ari Brown, M.D., author of Baby 411.

- **5 Days to Three Months**

Babies gain about an oz. each day on the average during this era or half a pound per week, they should be back to their birth weight by their second-week visit. Expect a growth surge around three weeks then another one at six weeks.

- **3 Months to Six Months**

A baby should gain about half a pound every fortnight. By six months, she should have doubled her birth weight.

- **7 Months to 12 Months**

A child would still gain about a pound a month. If you're nursing, your baby might not earn quite this much, or he may dip slightly from one percentile to a different on the expansion chart.

"At now, babies can also burn more calories because they're beginning to crawl or cruise," says Tanya Altman, M.D., a l. a. pediatrician and author of Mommy Calls. Even so, by the time he reaches his first birthday, expect him to possess grown 10 inches long and tripled his birth weight and his head to possess increased by about 4 inches.

Toddler Height and Weight Growth

- **Age 1**

Toddlers will grow at a slower pace this year but will gain half a pound a month and grow a complete of about 4 or 5 inches tall.

- **Age 2**

A kid will sprout about three more inches by the top of her third year and can have quadrupled her birthweight by gaining about four more pounds. By now, your pediatrician is going to be ready to make a reasonably accurate prediction about her adult height.

Preschooler Height and Weight Growth (Ages 3-4)

A preschooler will grow about 3 inches and gain 4 pounds annually.

You may also find that your child starts to shed the baby fat from his face and appears lankier since kids' limbs grow more by the time they're preschoolers, says

Daniel Rauch, M.D., professor of pediatrics at Sinai School of drugs, in NY City.

Kids Height and Weight Growth (Ages 5+)

Starting at five years old, kids will begin to grow about 2 inches and gain 4 pounds annually until puberty (usually between 8 and 13 for women and 10 and 14 for boys). Girls often reach their full height about two years after their period. Boys usually hit their adult height around age 17.

Happiness in Powerful

What Makes a toddler Happy?

We all want the equivalent things for our youngsters. We would like them to get older to enjoy and be loved, follow their dreams, and seek success. Mostly, though, we would like them to be happy. But just what proportion control can we have over our children's happiness?

Happy toddlers don't just happen...they're molded by parents who care!

Bubbling giggles, chubby feet, and colorful facial expressions all make-up a cheerful toddler! It thrills my soul to ascertain content. Well-loved toddlers explore their new world.

Their enthusiasm for lifestyle is contagious.

But some toddlers don't enjoy the blessings of a home that's crammed with encouraging words, bundles of hugs, and wheel barrels filled with kisses. Instead, they face daily criticism and harshness.

Have you ever heard a mother or father yell "Shut-up!" to their toddler?

Unfortunately, I even have. I shutter, and my teeth clench once I hear those anger-filled words. Rather than tearing toddlers down, we should always be encouraging them!

Our focus should be creating happy toddlers — not creating sad, frustrated, misunderstood toddlers! I'll admit it. Sometimes it's crazy-easy to bite off toddler because you're trying to get other work done and that they interrupt you once more.

- **Be present in your toddler's life**. Don't push your munchkin away once you are answering an email. Instead, please take a couple of moments and address her needs or wants. Take time to play together with your toddler a day. Make tents together, color pictures, continue walks, bake together, try these simple toddler activities, or whatever your child enjoys doing — do it! My youngest child enjoys swinging on our large patio swing. I attempt to make a "date" with him every day for this particular time. We are making memories!

- **Set goals**. Are you making dinner soon? Ask your toddler to assist set the table. Have you cleaned your room in the morning? Ask your baby to assist you in creating your bed. By giving toddlers responsibilities, you're letting them know they need an essential place in the family. When a toddler completes a goal, like chores, he begins to develop security and an "I can do it!" attitude.

It is my three-year-old son's task to open the door for visitors after they leave our home. He enjoys it so much! He always has an upbeat spirit when he runs back to us and can't wait to assist call at another area!

- **Establish boundaries**. Definite boundaries help a toddler understand what's acceptable in your home and what's not. If she doesn't know the principles, she will become paranoid and insecure about messing up. Make your rules reasonable and confirm you stick with them! If rules aren't enforced, they're worthless.

Examples of acceptable rules for toddlers:

- No whining or screaming.
- Say "please" and "thank-you."
- Pick up your toys after you play.
- Don't open the refrigerator.

As your child obeys these rules, she is going to feel confident that she is in a position to follow "house rules."

By establishing clear boundaries, you're promoting even more security for your toddler!

- **Praise often**. Criticism and negativity come from everywhere in the outside world. Create a haven in your home by praising your toddler for jobs well-done, good attitudes, or any positive characteristics you observe. Toasting a toddler always adds extra dashes of happiness to the soul!

- **Use eye contact**. When praising or correcting, get down on your toddler's eye level and speak one-on-one together. You're letting him know she is that the focus of your thoughts and energy. When he asks for a drink, squat down and ask him if he wants juice or milk. Take these extraordinary short conversations to interact together with your child to create his confidence in your unbiased love.

- **Smile often**. It is so easy to lose our smile when we're busy with daily tasks and life, isn't it? But a toddler finds much happiness in seeing a smile on mom's face. When a toddler sees that smile, the whole world looks like a peaceful, happy place...and the toddler knows that mom does love and look after him! Our face speaks a thousand words!

- **Listen**. Nothing says, "You don't matter," like someone not taking note of what you're saying. When your toddler gets excited about something and needs to point out and tell you about his discovery, really listen and concentrate. Discuss their discovery. Don't just say, "Uh. Yeah. That's neat. Now, go and play!" Your toddler knows when you're really listening and when you're just trying to shoo her away.

- **Laugh**! Go ahead, let your hair down and be super silly together with your toddler. Sing silly songs with them, talk in funny voices — anything to urge a smile or laugh from your kiddos. Adding some silliness and fun to your toddler's day is the perfect way to build them up!

- **Celebrate victories**! Did your toddler finally get the potty-training deal?! :) Did your toddler learn to successfully and routinely nap?! Those are HUGE milestones and will be celebrated! Celebrate with just a frozen dessert cone, a visit to the park, or some stickers! Please keep it simple, so it is often convenient to celebrate a replacement milestone in your munchkin's life.

If your toddler is battling napping successfully, we have an excellent super-loaded course for that! Yay for a toddler nap, right?!

Getting Started with Potty Training

Relax and know that development doesn't happen overnight. It's a process and takes time and practice to give desirable results.

Child-Centered Training

This theory was first advocated in the 1960s and revolved around the indisputable fact that potty training is hooked into the kid. Parents are there to point out by example but are never encouraged to push their child to start potty training. They will search for signs and provide their child with many opportunities to use the potty, but they should never force them into using it. With this concept, potty training might not happen until the kid is prepared when he turns 4.

Advocating For Diaper-Less Babies

Before the 1950s, diapers weren't used as often as they're today. Many advocates have observed that older generations started potty training earlier. They were more in tune with their elimination needs and sensations that accompany it. Once they pinpointed their child's cues and visual communication, they might sit him over the potty and make sounds like "sss" or say "pee-pee." The kid learns to travel about his business through active conditioning.

The best takeaway from these two different theories is that the mixture of them produces the simplest results. The primary child-centric approach gives credit to the child's feelings and independence. But without a guide to offer that tiny push, you'll be holding out on training for a way longer time as intended. By then, it's going instead be too late to start. The second theory relies on conditioning the tiny child over the to no matter his needs. The simplest way to approach this is often somewhere in the middle of those two theories.

When to Start Potty Training Your Child

There is no right age to bathroom train a toddler; the approximate time is between 15 months to 30 months.

Readiness to start potty training depends on the individual child. Generally, start before age 2 (24months) isn't recommended. The readiness skills and physical development your child needs occur between age 18 months and a couple of 5 years.

To understand how soon a toddler will start potty training, we glance at two development theories. These represent contrasting views on both ends of the spectrum.

Why it's Important to Potty Train Early

Potty training early has many advantages for you and your child. Potty training is a crucial part of your child's development. You should always strive to make your child's development your favorite priority, especially during their earliest years.

Potty training early will allow your child to feel some independence. It'll also give them great self-confidence and build up their self-esteem. They will be comfortable to go anyway with you knowing that they will go potty rather than being on an uncomfortable table to possess their diaper changed. Being potty trained does more for your child than keep them from wearing diapers. It gives them a way of accomplishment and self-worth.

Potty training early also will help your child's health. Diapers can cause nasty rashes and even yeast infections. While necessary, diapers aren't good for the skin or the body. The earlier your child can get out of diapers, the better.

There also are big perks for you once you potty train early. There's the obvious perk of not having to vary nasty diapers anymore. You don't need to smell diapers on your child while changing or child, or in the ashcan. Your whole house will smell better, and your family is going to be happier.

Diapers also are costly. A typical baby will undergo $840 worth of diapers in their first year. Once you begin buying bigger diapers and pull-ups, the value rises dramatically. The faster you get your child potty trained, the better it'll get on your pocketbook.

When you believe it, there are not any disadvantages to potty training at a young age. The advantages far outweigh any hassle you'll feel in browsing the method. However, if you undergo everything properly and prepare your child early, you'll not suffer much hassle in the least, and can only reap the advantages.

Debunking the Myths and Misconceptions of Potty Training

It's time to organize your child for a large milestone. Start by deconstructing the subsequent misconceptions below.

- **Myth 1: wait until your child gives you signals that he's ready**

This fact is false. To attend for signals is inviting all kinds of trouble. Your child has always peed into the diaper. He doesn't know that there's a world of potty out there. What signal could they provide once they don't know what to be signaling about?

The signals only come when potty training has begun. This way will be in the sort of a "pee-pee dance," which hopping from one foot to the opposite. This way is often an attempt to carry the pee. It could even be twitching or becoming angst or as simple as stating their need to use the potty.

Myth 2: girls are easier to coach than boys

Girls mature faster than boys; that's why the common consensus is that they're easier to coach. However, this is often not true. It's more hooked into how briskly a toddler learns as a private. This fact is often like learning to steer. A toddler could learn to control as early as 9 months or when he reaches 15 months. Each child is case dependent.

Myth 3: train them to pee first; only then are you able to train them to poop

This fact is false. Kids wouldn't know if the diaper he has on is for pooping or for peeing. The sole difference between the 2 acts would be the sensations they feel.

One of the items that do work is to let your child see how peeing and pooping is normal. Doing the act doesn't need to be a well-kept secret. It will sound unconventional but bringing your child with you to the potty is often a simple thing. While you are doing your stuff, have them sit and skim to them. Over time, your kid will realize that sitting on the potty seat may be a normal routine and isn't daunting.

Myth 4: put the potty seat out before you start training so that they're going to get used to it

This fact is false. Putting out a potty seat for the kid to get conversant with is counterproductive. The child will start to urge it confused together with his toys if it's

30

in plain sight. If he's used to seeing it daily, he might not put any thought into the seriousness of its function.

The ABC of Potty Training

There are no specific steps required to be followed when potty training, but using the alphabet can help you recollect the essential principles that make potty training tons easier and simpler.

Assessment

Make sure your child is prepared for potty training. Not only that, confirm you're able to undergo the system also. A part of the assessment and readiness is to make sure there are no significant events or stressful situations like getting into a replacement house or transferring to a replacement school.

Buying Equipment

Many places cater to everyone's potty training needs. The key is to settle on equipment that matches the budget, is comfortable and suitable for your child, and is compatible with your current lifestyle situation.

Demonstrations

Children are stimulated visually and learn fast by imitation. Allowing them to observe you attend the bathroom and use the potty will help them know what it's all about.

Tell your child how to know the time to use the potty.

Explain what you're doing while in the bathroom.

Let your child see what you "made" before showing how you wipe or wash yourself.

Let your child see how your pull-up your underwear and pants, how you flush, and the way you wash your hands after.

Note: If your child has potty trained siblings, it's a simple idea to allow them to do an indication also. Seeing children on the brink of their age using the potty or potty can also encourage your child to do it.

Knowing If Your Child is prepared

Many parents plan to start potty training when their toddler begins showing interest in the potty. However, since you've built up this interest over time, this is often not an adequate measurement.

Taking Off Pull-Ups

If they take it off as soon as they need to peed or pooped, it's a sure sign that they need to obviate that diaper. The child notices that it's uncomfortable to put on a wet or dirty diaper and that they don't want to put it on at all once this happens. So, they're going to take it off immediately. Not eager to wear pull-ups may be a good indication that they will be willing to use the potty for that added advantage.

Telling You They Have Gone

Suppose your child comes and tells you as soon as they have gone potty in their have a pull-up, they're likely to potty train. If they tell you as soon as they have gone, ought to be ready to begin telling you before they are going. At now, they likely know what it seems like. Once they need to go and are only waiting to inform you until after the event so that they don't need to sit in it. This ability to understand once they need to go potty is a crucial trait that must occur before you potty train.

Wanting to Wipe Themselves

Many toddlers begin eagerly to wipe themselves in a diaper change. This way shows you that your child is prepared for a few independence. Your toddler wants to start doing things for themselves, rather than counting on you entirely. While this concept may cause you to be sad to see your child growing up, it's a moral development and one that naturally results in potty training.

Seating Dolls On the Potty

Many toddlers introduced to the potty early will begin putting their dolls or stuffed animals on the potty. They could even say that "Buddy" goes potty. They could tell that he's an honest boy for going potty. Toddlers tend to act out the items they understand and need to do through imaginary play with toys. If your child begins to do this with their dolls or stuffed animals, they're ready and quite willing to use the potty themselves.

Potty Training Checklist

There are some benchmarks that the kid can clear faster than others. The list below shows a number of the foremost common behaviors your child exhibits when he's potty trained. Confine mind that each child is different, and yours may produce other ways of letting you recognize.

Between the age of 18 months to three years, your child will reach the purpose of muscle control that creates it possible for self-regulation. You'll enhance the probabilities of him succeeding in his potty-training journey at around 18-24 months old. Other indicators, like the cues and his interest in using the potty, will prompt you to start. You want to await the signs of readiness.

Keep tabs on your child's elimination habits. After a meal, note how long it takes for him to pee or has a bowel movement. once you start potty-training, this timing data are often useful to steer him to his potty seat. Once you can time the potty moment when he's very likely feeling the urge, then you'll expect much better results. With this method, you're also trying to work out when he will get to go so that you'll sit him on the potty and make the deposit in the bowl rather than the diaper.

Steps and Rules for the Potty Training

Assess Your Child's Readiness For Potty Training

Potty training readiness takes a child-oriented approach because the youngsters, not the old ones, take the lead. Some parents make the error of pushing their children into training before they're ready, and that they find yourself scaring and traumatizing their children so that the method is delayed further. Since children cannot speak up or understand the changes in their bodies, parents should keep an eye fixed on the signs their children give to assess the children's readiness to start potty training.

Make Potty-Training Preparations

The first thing to do is to organize your child psychologically so that he or she understands what you're about doing about. Inform them what potty training is, letting them know the difference between

36

pee and poop. Sometimes, the most crucial shock for teenagers is to ascertain stuff beginning of their bodies, especially if they have been in diapers all day. Show your child videos and books of various characters using the potty to awaken their interest. You'll even demonstrate with some dolls or allow the kid to ascertain you and, therefore, the siblings using the potty. Let the kid see that this is often normal.

Your child will get as excited as you always are when someone takes you for shopping. Gestures like these make an individual feel wanted and valued, and your child will feel these emotions. Therefore, as you set about preparing for potty training, involve the kid in every step. For instance, walk to the shop, and let the kid choose a potty in their favorite color. Once you're home, allow the kid to play together with his potty, sit on it, and do all types of activities that would help make a positive association between the kid and its potty.

Some parents choose the potty seat rather than the potty. We feel that the potty is simpler to use, which can often be moved around the house, concerning the child's preferences. The training seat is nice too, but it'll require you to buy for a footstep so that your child can have a platform to put his legs for stability. The step also allows the kid to urge to and from the potty seat independently.

While some experts recommend having your child go bare-bottomed a day until the kid can voluntarily use the potty, some think that a pair of underwear is sweet enough. If you select the underwear or the training pants path, you would like to stack many of them because your child will get to change whenever accidents occur.

Cloth training pants are a bit like regular pants; they only need a pad that absorbs fluid whenever accidents occur. Trainer pants are comfortable to tug up and down, and while some parents find them helpful, others find them almost like a cloth nappy. If the training pants are still an uncomfortable idea, choose the underwear because it's light and straightforward to figure up and down. As you shop, have your kid choose underwear together with his favorite cartoon characters drawn on them.

Also, have many wet wipes and other cleaning supplies to wash the messes once they occur. Most significantly, have two or three potty chairs, and scatter all of them around your home rather than dedicating them in one room only.

Another way to urge your child hospitable the potty idea is to encourage the kid familiar with staying clean and dry weeks before. Let your child get familiar with wearing only clean diapers or clean pants by teaching your kid to invite changes whenever they soiled his diapers. Once a toddler learns about this privilege, they will be hospitable, doing anything to maintain a dry environment.

Be Consistent In Your Approach to Potty Training

Children depend upon consistency to find out anything new, and to urge your child to require up the potty, and you'll need to be slow and consistent in your approach. As we've acknowledged in the previous section, once you buy the potty, please don't force your child onto it immediately; allow the kid to interact with it and know its use. Let the kid sit thereon and obtain comfortable.

You need to stay reminding the kid about the potty a day and ask him to take a seat thereon, perhaps after breakfast or before a shower or at the standard time the kid poops. Roll in the hay when the kid has had a wet diaper to strengthen where the pee and therefore the poop should go. In this way, your child will be used to the potty and start to receive it as a part of his day. take

If the kid is interested and manages to use the potty correctly, be happy. Don't expect an equivalent success next time and negatively act when he misses. Take every trial as a separate attempt and twiddling my thumbs. Encourage him that peeing and pooping at the proper place may be a grown-up thing. Every child wants to feel significant, and your child will begin to make an attempt to act grown all the time. The worst thing you'll do is become frustrating and switch the training experience into a battleground.

Ensure that anyone else who takes care of your child understands what you're doing and how to do it so that the kid's experience is consistent throughout the day. Daycare staff, sitters, grandparents, aunties, older siblings, and each other relative who helps should take an equivalent approach. Have them learn the teachings you've got haunted and make sure that they persistently make potty training a stimulating activity for your child.

Get to find out your child's pace of learning and stick with it. As a parent, you'll feel as if you would like to stretch your child's ability, but remember that everything you're doing is sort of new to him. Also, every child is different. If your first child had been potty trained at 24 months, your second child might take longer and even get to 4 years. Whatever it takes, maintain a cheerful and positive environment because it's the critical motivator on this journey.

Demonstrate How It's Done

Everything must be taught, and therefore the best way to teach a toddler is through demonstration. Demonstration makes everything about potty training appear more natural and normal for the kid.

The reality is it's getting to weird you out! Most hate being close to another person in the potty, and therefore the idea of getting your child with you in the potty feels downright strange. Fortunately, there are other techniques to demonstrate this without making it weird for those involved.

The demonstration must begin with information. Begin by lecture your toddler about how it feels when it's time to urge into the potty. This way will be easy if your child sees you do these things, but if it's not your thing, don't fret because you'll still demonstrate the method using props. What's more, you'll be there when your kid goes through the technique, and you'll guide him through it.

The primary technique involves employing a doll. The doll will assist you to demonstrate the whole process leading up to the potty. Begin with you and your kid giving the toy something to drink, then say that the doll wants to travel pee. Help the toy pull down its pants and help it sit on the potty. By doing this, you'll be modeling the behavior you would like your kid to require. It also gives your child authority over the doll going potty, creating a way of responsibility, and a willingness to master the technique before using it for themselves later. By the time the kid does it himself, he will feel more confident about the method.

The second technique is to outsource. Find relations or friends who have a child a little older than yours and is already potty trained. Let your kid enter the potty with the opposite kid to observe what's being done. Kids wish to learn from one another, and little question seeing it firsthand will help your kid learn the technique much faster.

The third technique involves printing out the instructions you would like your kid to follow and arranging them in a sequence. Some people print out words, but in our case, we advocate that you simply print out photos indicating each of the actions you desire your kid to require as he or she goes to the restroom. A child's memory improves through visual aids instead of reading. Print out pictures, and ask your child to demonstrate to you what's happening. If possible, stick the photos to the potty wall or an area where the kid can see as he sits on the potty. The photographs are going to be an excellent demonstration and a reminder of what must be done.

Just like that, you'll have taught your child the way to go potty!

Persevere With the Potty If He's Ready

Potty training is merely possible if your child is ready; if they aren't prepared, it'll be a battle all day long. Things get worse if your child is that stubborn kind, the type you simply need to fight and argue with about everything. If your child isn't ready, let the training plan rest for a few weeks before you revisit the difficulty. If your child is prepared, plow ahead and use the potty a day.

Ensure that you encourage the kid to use the potty whenever the urge comes on. For the primary few days, make sure that the kid has plenty to drink and obtain them to take a potty seat every half-hour to an hour. Let the kid know that he can let you know whenever the urge comes and assure him of your company whenever he visits the restroom.

Therefore, on your part, be able to abandon what you're doing at the time. While the kid may require your help in the primary days, the "big boy" attitude will kick in soon, and therefore the child will want to do everything by himself.

One tricky issue about this first part of the method is that your child might consider it a hassle. It's an opportunity from the norm, and as you recognize, no change is straightforward. You'll need to keep reminding the kid to travel to the potty. If you depend upon the child's opinion, be assured of an emphatic "no" and pee after five minutes. For this reason, let the initiative come from you; persuade your child to travel potty by saying something like, "Go and pee, then we will eat some frozen dessert," or "Go poop so that we will attend the mall." Give the kid some persuasion to start the training, and shortly enough, because the child enjoys the comfort that comes with emptying the bowels, he will go potty on his own accord.

Some toddlers are so active and can't sit on the potty long enough to end their business. In a case like this, calmly encourage your child to take a seat and wait some minutes. Make the kid aware of what's happening by asking if anything is "coming out." The kid will begin giving some thought to the method, and every one his concentration is going to be on what he's doing. Another strategy is to talk to the kid some calming words or read him a story. Your child is going to be calm, and therefore the chances of success will rise.

If the method is successful, shower your child with praise, but don't go overboard. You'll give him a treat. Nobody likes to perform under stress. Instead, only praise him enough for him to understand that using the potty instead of the diaper, or messing his pants, is sort of an accomplishment.

Cope Calmly with Potty Training Accidents

Potty training tends to be as stressful to a toddler because it is to its parents. The rationale it becomes daunting for the oldsters is probably they need to wait for it for quite a while, or they compare the kid's learning to that of other children. Other times, it might be because your child has been doing so well, and every one of a sudden, the kid is back to using the potty on himself. To avoid getting overwhelmed and transferring your frustration to your child, know that mistakes are sure to happen during potty training, even once you think the method has been a hit. Therefore, enter it with this data because if you expect it, you won't be too surprised when it happens.

The reason mistakes like those happen is that the sensors in the child's body are yet to develop fully, making it hard for them to work out correctly when their bladders or bowels are full. You see, it's not the child's fault; the difficulty is that his or her feelings aren't there yet. What's more, albeit you become upset, you'll not change anything about the situation; you'll only make it worse by causing the kid to become self-conscious. If the kid learns that accidents are intolerable to you, the kid will begin to carry the pee or poop instead, recoil from using the potty, and demand using diapers.

You see, once the training process begins, reverting to diapers would be an enormous mistake. If you're certain that the kid is prepared, then he's ready. If he's not, cease the training. Getting back to diapers for a ready toddler deteriorates their learning because the developing consciousness is buried again. Therefore, if you would like your child to find out, let the kid know that accidents can happen sometimes, but they must try harder to avoid repeating the error. Encourage the kid to speak better with you next time, and if the kid is sufficiently old, ask him or her to wash up the mess.

Cleaning up isn't harsh at all; it only strengthens the message that using the potty is far better than allowing the accident to happen. Cleaning doesn't mean that you hand the kid a bucket of water and a mop, like Cinderella; you'll ask the kid to tug down the dirty underwear or pants and put it in the clothes hamper; otherwise, you could hand him a rag and ask him to wipe the pee.

Be prepared that even when the kid has nailed the day potty routine, they should need a diaper in the night. Don't ask the kid to wash up then. Only ask the kid to travel to the restroom the last item before getting to bed to extend a dry diaper's probabilities in the morning.

If the accidents happen once you are far away from home, be calm about things, too. Quickly rush your child to a potty or a restroom so he can finish going and pack up the remainder of the mess soon to avoid drawing attention to yourself so that the child is often as comfortable as possible readjusting after the accident. The lesser attention you pull, the quicker you progress from the incident.

The Basics of Potty Training

Potty Training for Boys

Most experts, like the Mayo Clinic doctors, suggest that you simply should await your child to coach potty. There are signs of readiness to be interested in the potty, the power to stay in a dry place for a couple of hours, complain about dirty clothes, follow simple directions, and tug his pants alone.

Kids hit these preparation stages at various times, and boys are somehow slower than girls specifically. This fact does not mean that when your daughter started, you cannot introduce the potty at age 2. And only that he might not have an interest until the age of three or later. Pressure tends to steer to resentment and poor results.

It's fundamental physiology, Boy Potty Basics. Your son's penis at this age is simply a little seed. There's not much to hold up, and it's only a small standing up when it's filled with pee. This way often results in a little (or significant) mess when the potty is employed. You discover many have a "splash guard" to stop these messes if you get a potty or insert a daily potty. It's sort of a good idea, but not always. If it's a rotating sprinkler instead of something built right into the chair, it can unintentionally pinch the genitalia as he sits down or stands up. You'll easily imagine how this might affect your potty workouts.

Nevertheless, as are often seen, by the likelihood of pinching and, therefore, the possible mess, it's essential to start to take a seat right down to avoid even bigger messes. You had the sensation of walking into the potty, thinking that you just had to pee, which isn't it all?

Your son should even be ready to see people who attend the potty. Dad's best, but if he isn't going, roll in the hay with other men or boys. As he looks at people in the bathroom, he will see that they're standing up.

The "easy potty-training techniques" (as in the way your child is potty training in a few days) usually revolve around your child spending some naked time in the house, making it quicker and easier for him to urge to the restroom. However, it requires additional diligence these few days because it is essential to ascertain him for signs that he must go and help make sure that he reaches the potty on time.

Either way, many parents will find that some reward system works well. As an example, you'll use a sticker chart or tell him you'll buy a coveted toy after a particular number of days of successful potting.

Ultimately, your son wants to start peeing back just like the big boys. Which may be the day things get tousled. When it involves peeing up, young boys (check, even older men) don't always have an ideal aim. I conclude that a two-fold approach is the best way to address this issue.

Next, you would like him to specialize in his target. Throw some marks into the restroom and check out to hit them. This way might be a couple of cereal products; otherwise, you can purchase specially designed potty targets. Setting goals produces a challenge that will help him get excited about doing it right.

The main thing you've got to do is confirm the cleanses himself. It's no harm to your son to point out that he should take a little potty tissue once he's finished peeing to wipe out any drops round the bowl or on the ground. Explain the case, but an enormous boy cleanses it. He should also put down the restroom, flush the potty, and wash his hands. Once you make this stuff an integral component of the restroom routine, it'll be done automatically, and therefore the bathroom will be cleaner.

How To Potty Train A Boy Successfully

Use the subsequent checklist to trace the progress of your child in this learning process. You do not need to await every item to be checked to place your boy in the pot! See if your baby appears to be more self-sufficient or if he or she knows what it means to go to the potty like an adult.

The child can begin the pot if it's standard, pulled, or handmade stools.

Will remove and restore the painting.

Is capable of imitating the practices of others in the potty (if he sees you attend a potty, then he wants to wear underwear)

The manifestation of the way to pee or poo

Could obey simple directions (like "give me this toy") Recognizes the physical sign.

Let him watch and learn when your boy gets potty training. The youngsters learn by imitation. After his dad, aunt, or family friend watching him in the potty, you'll encourage your boy to urge to understand the thought. He may note that mom and pop don't use the bathtub equally. This way provides you the prospect to elucidate how little boys pee.

If you select to get a restroom stabilizer to place on your potty, confirm it's secure and cozy. If you go that option, you've got to shop for a stool; therefore, the child can move down and up the restroom easily when he needs it and support his legs when sitting. This book explaining the way to use the potty is another right way of learning.

Begin by making him understand that he belongs to its potty or potty chair. You'll personalize it by inserting his name or allowing it to be decorated with stickers. You'll recommend him to get rid of his shorts, underwear, or diaper every week later. Don't pressure him if he refuses. This way may only create an influence balance that might deregulate the whole process. Use it to show your child the way to enter the bathtub if you've got a favorite doll or toy. Children wish to see a favorite toy of theirs wake up, and therefore the explanation has more effect than if it came from them. Some mothers even make doll potty, so everyone has their potty!

Draw your son's eye to the gains of cleaning him by getting him to possess a singular shopping experience: his first underwear! Tell him he can choose what he wants (pants or boxers always very successful with the cartoon characters or superheroes).

If you would like somebody else responsible for your child while you're in business, you will have to offer the kindergarten staff or nanny your strategy. You've got to settle on between the diapers and, therefore, the underwear. When wearing a diaper is practical, most experts and fogeys like better to put children in washable clothing so that the baby is instantly damp.

Of furthermore, just in case of accidents, you'll get to pack up. Ask your pediatrician if you cannot choose a method. For a time, disposable pairs of pants will still be used in the dark and long journeys.

Teach him to take a seat down and get up as poo and pee often happens simultaneously, teaching your son first to take a seat and understand that everything goes into the pot makes more sense. And thus, he won't attempt to play and aim, while he should focus exclusively on mastering cleanliness basics. If your son is relaxed on his pot or potty, consider him standing on his tiny stool so that it's at its right height.

Potty Training for Girls

There is no actual training age. However, the typical age most parents begin potty training their girls is between the ages of two and three. If your daughter has older siblings, she may learn much before a firstborn.

Whichever the case, you ought to plan your training wisely, explicitly choosing the time when no significant changes are happening in your child's environment. If there are substantial changes in the household, wait until she settles down and not feels overwhelmed, then begin the training.

If she is at the stage where she says "no" to everything you ask of her, including potty training, remind yourself that she is merely in a phase that will be receptive to new things once she is through with it. You need to delay the potty training until the way step is over.

Potty Training Equipment

The first step here is to get the potty chair or the potty seat and make sure that the kid knows that it's hers. This way could happen once you notice the signs of readiness, although the training will begin weeks, if not months later. Allow the kid to interact with the potty and find out how it's used. Encourage your child to personalize the potty by writing her name thereon or placing some sparkly stickers.

Your baby will likely feel more comfortable training on a potty seat than using the restroom seat directly. You see, children have a natural fear of falling, and since the restroom is raised high above the bottom, the kid will fear to fall to the side, falling on the steps, or falling into the water when seated. It doesn't help that some seats fidget and don't stick firmly to the large chair.

Everything that a toddler uses must be children-friendly. It should be safe, comfortable, and fun. A nice potty seat is one that your child can sit on comfortably, move around the house, and sit or rise from it with ease. Besides comfort and security, a potty seat is advantageous because the kid can use it outside of the potty, and therefore the parent can empty the contents in the potty.

You see, bathrooms are dangerous places even for grown-ups, and to possess a toddler to enter one without supervision when she uses the restroom would be quite risky. Therefore, as you buy, choose a comfy light potty seat that she will use unsupervised if you would like your child to cultivate some independence not to need to be there or worry whenever she wants to pee.

Since there are some excellent potty-training seats in the market, if your child isn't afraid, get her one, and make sure that you create the experience as easy for her as you'll. Make sure that the seat is secure, comfy, attaches firmly, and doesn't pinch. Get a stool to make it easier to urge to the highest of the restroom bowl.

Ensure that you furthermore may stock a spread of fun things your daughter can enjoy while using the potty. Stock some picture books; otherwise, you could download a potty-training app for your child to entertain your daughter as she eases herself.

How to Start Potty Training

The best learning avenue for youngsters is via imitation. It's easier for them to do what you are doing than for them to follow instructions together with your mouth. You'll spend tons of your time explaining the potty procedure, and your child won't understand what's happening, but if you demonstrate it, she will understand and start to repeat what you are doing in no time. Therefore, don't close the door once you enter to use the restroom. Leave it open and provides your child the chance to ascertain how it's done.

If daddy does an equivalent and doesn't lock the potty door, your child will make a transparent distinction that daddy pees standing up while mummy pees seated. When this happens, take this chance to elucidate the mechanics behind boys peeing standing up and girls doing it while seated. Tell her that girls and their mommies need to pee sitting.

If she needs a little help, demonstrate how it's done using her favorite stuffed animal or doll. Hopefully, she is going to realize that using the potty is normal and relatively easy.

If your daughter still doesn't sit on the potty despite your calm efforts, avoid pressuring her because which will be the start of the facility struggle, which will further derail the training process.

How to Motivate Her to Use the Potty

The way to get your daughter all excited about potty training is by taking her on a memorable trip to the emporium to shop for her own potty and knickers. Get her some knickers with special designs and her favorite cartoon characters. Also, make sure that the knickers are comfortable, ensuring that your child will enjoy wearing them.

Personalize the potty or seat by allowing them to embellish it with some stickers or writing on its sides with some glitter glue. They could use the glue to make interesting patterns. After this, have her sit on the chair with clothes on for practice. Doing this stuff should get your child excited about becoming an enormous girl who can now use grown-up stuff.

The way to build up the thrill is to plan the trip. Get her talking about it a day, and when she does something good round the house or behaves well, let her know that you simply will give her a gift once you take her to shop for some "big girl stuff" just like the potty and therefore the knickers. Tell her that she will start to be like her elder sisters or like mommy when you begin the training. Keep the hope and excitement alive so that once you finally make the trip, your child is going to be quite excited about purchasing and using the potty-training stuff.

How Can She Recognize the Signs of Wanting to Wee?

Your female child will need to determine when she must attend the potty by herself. You'll keep reminding her at the start of the training, but she needs to be sensitive enough to understand when she needs a wee with time. The way to cultivate this sensitivity is to possess your child to spend some considerable time during the day with none underwear. This way often is so that when the pee comes gushing out, the kid will feel and see it flow so that whenever the sensation comes, she will associate it with wetness, and she or he will rush to seek out the potty.

The potty should be in your child's reach. Ensure that space between the potty and the area where the kid is playing is near so that she will get to that in time. With that said, be ready for the occasional puddles when the kid cannot urge the potty and when she is unable to take a seat on the potty seat properly, leading to some liquid drops to the ground.

Have some cleaning agents, like a carpet cleaner, at hand; otherwise, you could cover your carpet with some plastic to stay it from absorbing the fluids.

When to Praise Her During Potty Training

Children like to know that they need their parents' support and approval altogether they are doing. They wish to make their parents proud and receive recognition and praise in exchange. Your female child is like that. She wants to understand that she makes you cheerful and proud as she learns how to use the potty. Praise also will let her know that she is stepping into the "big girl" league a bit like mom and, therefore, the elder sisters. This fact may be a dream come true for her because toddlers wish to consider themselves as adults, adequate to their mothers, and other more senior people in the house.

When your daughter eventually gets something in her potty, celebrate this tremendous success. Shower her with praise, telling her how confident she was, how happy she looked, and the way grown-up her actions were. Give her a gift, possibly a sticker of her favorite cartoon character, her favorite food, a cookie, some juice, and the other thing your child fancies. If she loves bedtime stories, promise to read her an additional one as she goes to bed in the night, and make sure that you retain your promise.

As we've discussed, don't go overboard together with your praise and rewards; don't make an enormous deal of her potty use. Make it appear as a standard event but make sure that your daughter feels appreciated and encouraged to do the proper thing. Take care that an excessive amount of attention could make your child self-conscious, anxious, and afraid to use the potty again.

When To Banish Nappies

A child will learn and persist with any skill because it is consistently presented in her environment. Suppose potty training is always practiced so that the parent, nanny, and caregivers at the daycare are a coordinated team who uses an equivalent potty-training approach.

In that case, your child will learn the skill much quicker.

The best approach to training is to modify from using diapers to underwear all day, from the very beginning. This way, there'll be no switching methods in the middle of the training, and your child won't be confused. You'll also take up the utilization of pull-up training pants. Still, experts agree that it's the washable cotton training pants that produce the simplest experience because your daughter is going to be aware of her wetness immediately when an accident happens. Be prepared that there'll be several accidents before the kid fully masters the utilization of the potty.

Whenever you're out, carry with you some clean knickers, pair of tights, and a few trousers, even once you are only taking a brief trip to the shop. If you allow your child at a daycare or preschool once you attend work during the day, make sure that you allow a giant stack of the things your daughter may need during the day. Once you leave your child under the care of a nanny or a sitter, make sure that they need quick access to the other clothes too. If you would like advice and recommendations on the way to keep it up the training stress-free, ask other moms in your playgroup to seek out how they solve a number of the challenges they encounter. Remember, though, that each child is different and requires a singular approach. Whenever you would like to undertake something new, ask your child's pediatrician first.

Weeing, Pooping, and Preventing Infection

For girls, even wiping takes a selected strategy. Teach her that she needs to wipe from the front to the rear whenever she uses the potty, especially if she had a poo. This way is often a healthy practice that keeps bacteria from the bowel spreading into the vagina areas and, therefore, the urethra. If they have difficulty stretching their hand to effectively wipe front to back, opt that they pat themself dry after peeing, and when they poop, she should involve assistance to wipe.

It is not uncommon to ascertain a case of a tract infection (UTI) in a child, especially girls. The condition develops when the kid holds in urine for too long. And when bowel bacteria get to the vagina and proceed to the urethra.

UTIs in children are identified through the following signs. The primary is that the kid will begin to complain of some pain whenever she pees or some discomfort around the pelvis or tummy region. The second sign is that each one of a sudden, the girl will begin to wet her pants, even after successful potty training and having achieved reasonable bladder control. The third sign is that the kid will develop a requirement to pee more often, and typically, the acute urge to pee comes suddenly. If you notice any of those signs in your child, rush her to a hospital to possess her treatment.

Making Potty Training Fun

Making potty training fun is all about arising with things that your daughter can anticipate to. For instance, rewards are ideal for once you notice that your child is beginning to lose interest in potty training while she is well into it. You'll offer the girl a glittery sticker whenever she uses her potty correctly. Ask her to place the stickers onto a wall chart to ascertain how far the rewards go before the kid is totally potty trained. Seeing the rewards chart also will encourage her to continue doing her best. It builds confidence because when the kid sees just what percentage of successful potty trips she has made, she will think that she has grown up and is rightfully acting like a grown-up.

Once she has been ready to stay dry for several consecutive days, leave together with your daughter and treat her to that toy or dress, she has longed for. Some girls love jewelry, too. Know what makes your child happy, and when she has behaved so well, it provides it to her to strengthen the excellent behavior.

When Will Nights Be Dry Too?

When you have successfully potty trained your daughter so that she stays dry all day, turn your attention to the nighttime training. Whenever she takes naps or wakes up in the morning, check her diaper to ascertain whether or not they remained dry while the kid was asleep. If the diaper turns up dry for several nights in a row, your child is prepared for nighttime potty training.

By the time children get to 4 years, many of them are yet to master the skill of staying dry while they sleep. Therefore, don't be worried if your daughter still cannot remain dry. Just confine mind that it takes longer, which it's a little harder to coach for the nighttime. This way is often because this type of coaching requires that the child's bladder be entirely developed so that it can hold pee for long hours as your baby sleeps. Also, your child is just too young to take note of bladder sensations when it must be emptied. For these reasons, it's of absolute importance that you simply wait a short time until your daughter has had several dry nights before beginning the nighttime training.

If your child insists that she is prepared to sleep without the diapers, allow her. The mornings then are going to be those to work out whether she is ready to entirely ditch diapers or not. If she is yet to be prepared, gracefully switch back to diapers without having to make your child as she failed herself otherwise. Inform her that her body must grow and gain the capacity to carry pee for therefore long. Reassure her though it won't be long until she is large enough to offer potty training another shot.

Kindly don't plan to reduce your daughter's intake during the day. During the day, she needs to take six to eight cups of fluid. Also, at home, avoid taking drinks that contain caffeine before she goes to bed.

Signs that a Toddler is Already Potty-Trained

- **They already know, and that they tell you if their underwear is wet**

The very sign that a toddler is already potty-trained or is getting there's if they know they need wet their underwear. This way is often a symbol that they are already hygienic, and that they know that they need to travel somewhere to pee or poop, not just in their underwear.

- **They want to get their rewards**

Why? Because they know that what they're doing are some things right, and that wants to prove that they're learning.

When a toddler learns the ideas of rewards and positive reinforcement, they start to possess that healthy competitive streak in them. This way is often something good because it shows that they'd get rewarded if they understand what you're trying to show them. They know their 'rewards if they are doing something right, so in fact, they're going to work on doing that.

- **They go to the potty seat and check out, especially once they desire they need to pee or poop**

Another big sign that they are learning is when they go to their chair and try going potty. For one, the children need to please you; and they also know that this is often right. And once the children attempt to do what's right, it means they're learning, and you're doing something right.

- **They're pleased with their new underpants**

When they want to select new underpants, it means they know children are not a baby, and since they are not a "baby," they're going to be skilled about their pee and poop!

Potty Training in the Dark

Staying dry in the dark while typically sleeping takes longer than staying dry in awake time. Sometimes, children don't master this skill until they're between ages five and seven. Until then, you'll reduce frustration by buying mattress covers to guard their beds. Disposable training pants are another great option—they make some designed to be larger for bigger kids. These contain significant accidents and are designed to be comfortable.

Even if your child continues to possess an occasional accident, many are ready to know they need to pee, wake up, and use the restroom by the age of 4. This fact often is because there's a nerve that sends a sign to the brain when their body must use the potty, causing the kid to awaken. Bladder size and, therefore, the ability to carry back urine also are significant factors to success.

Here are a couple of things that you simply should confine mind:

Encourage your child to use the potty before lying down, albeit they insist they are doing not need to go. This way may reduce the probabilities that they're going to rise and use the restroom a couple of hours after lying down.

Make sure that the way to the potty is well lit. If your child wakes up and is scared to travel to the potty alone, he or she may wet the bed, so that they don't need to walk down the scary hallway.

Limit what proportion your child drinks before he or she lies down for the night. You'll decide what your child supports these limits. Consider letting them have a little drink after dinner, then just a sip of water before bed.

Wake your child up before you lie for the night. Often, parents stay awake later than their children to end up the day's tasks (or finally enjoy the quiet). If this is often the case in your family, wake your child up to use the restroom before you head to bed.

Do not get upset about accidents. Children are very perceptive to hear sighs and see your visual communication once you are upset and become discouraged. Be happy for them and offer praise once they awaken dry but try not to be upset once you need to wash their bedsheets. Clean them up, offer a change of garments, and then pack up the mess as if it's no big deal.

Children take a while to transfer the success of the day training to the night. Even when the kid has been successfully dry all day, remaining dry through the night could take some months or years. Therefore, once the times are dry, don't throw the diapers away entirely. The child's body will make yet develop the consciousness it must wake him in the night to attend to the potty.

For most kids, night training begins once they are 3 to 4 years old when the kid has started wake up with a dry diaper for several mornings in a row. If you start the training before then, make sure that you've got a pad or an absorbent sheet on the bed to avoid wetting the mattress.

While many fluids aid day training, night training requires on the brink of no fluids in the night. Make sure that your child doesn't take any drinks just before bedtime. Some parents limit the drinks to six pm, but confirm that the kid is well hydrated during the day by taking 6 to 7 cups of drink. Keep offering the drinks because some children become too absorbed in playing and cannot invite any.

The training process may appear to be difficult for your child but be assured that your child can handle it. If the kid is prepared and willing to find out, he will. You're only required to stay calm and lend a hand, and therefore the rest will follow. Only confirm not to force a toddler who cannot undergo it because if you are doing, you'll only have yourself responsible.

Reinforcing Success

Do not expect a toddler to make the connection between sitting on a potty and eliminating it. He can only recognize a pattern when he gets praise from you. Another very effective way is to line up a hit chart where you'll both track his progress.

Kids love stickers. Having a hit chart where she will put stickers on can boost her motivation. Make an enormous deal about her getting stickers. Whenever she is in a position to eliminate, you'll give her a sticker. However, expect slip-ups to happen. Rather than a sticker, you'll give her verbal praise. Reassure her that she may get the sticker on her next potty successful trip. You're giving her something to seem forward to, together with her being motivated to succeed and obtain her badge of honor.

Giving out physical rewards or prizes also works, as does making good on a promise. You'll tell your child that if she will poop in the potty and fail afterward, you'll both visit the park later in the afternoon. Toddlers and youngsters who are active would love this type of reward because it allows them to do what they like best.

If your child rebels and asserts her stance not to use the potty or potty, don't take this to heart an excessive amount. It is often frustrating but exercises extended patience. Children are just testing you for backlash. Don't concede. Instead, smile and check out, saying the things below. A younger child who is more resistant may have a special quite incentive, one that's only reserved after she goes for a restroom break.

Do not show any adverse reactions to the smell, consistency, amount, or appearance of her stool or pee. This way, she is going not to be ready to associate bowel movements as something to be ashamed of, but rather as a part of a traditional bodily process.

Potty training may be a time where you ought to be slathering on praises as often and the maximum amount as you'll. Keep rewarding the child for the milestones – his potty sitting effort, the way he removes his underpants, flushing the restroom, and for laundry her hands right after. Clap your hands, hug her, and make her desire she's a star. Tell him that eliminating his waste is that the stuff that super cool kids do is often a bit like his parents.

The next challenge is for you to stay the great habits ingrained during the entire process. Joining forces with other members of your family and other caregivers (teachers, day school watchers) will help cultivate in her a real-world approach to elimination. Gradually decrease the praises but keep them coming. Once your child has found his groove, reinforce it. The fanfare should settle down by this point but be consistent in letting her know that he's doing an excellent job in which you're pleased with him. Make refresher comments now then, and check out to stay the momentum going. Let him know that assistance is there if he needs it. If you're not around, he can seek help from other adults and grown-ups like his grandparents, his teachers, or his siblings.

An ideal outcome is when the kid feels a way of pride in himself and not fear. Confirm he isn't unsure of himself, which may cause regression when he's placed in a stressful situation.

Taking Control

The biggest hurdle for toddlers learning to potty train is understanding what's required to control their bodies. These sensations are hard to explain and understand for a toddler.

Bladder Control

Summertime may be a blast to start potty training because clothes are lighter and easier to urge off. When children have accidents, it's easier to wash those clothes also. Once you begin bladder control training, you would like to devote three days in a row to the present and supply complete specialize in the kid at this point. You'll get to be accessible to attend to the kid immediately when they have got to participate in the potty.

You want to elucidate to the kid what you're expecting before you begin training. You would like the kid to possess the maximum amount of ownership over the potty-training process as possible. There are some ways to assist confirm that the potty-training experience is about up for fulfillment. The primary thing to do is to make sure that the kid is placed in the restroom around sleeping. This fact suggests very first thing in the morning, before and after naps, and before bedtime. Also, confirm that you simply attempt to use the restroom after two hours of being dry. This way may provide a schedule that will offer you the simplest chance of success.

When the kid is in the restroom, keep them company so that it's not so scary. Ask them or read to them so that they do something else at an equivalent time. Otherwise, they'll be inclined not to use the potty because they might preferably be doing something else.

Praise the kid for employment well done. This fact is often actual for any small milestone. If they sit in the restroom for quite ten seconds, praise them. You'll help them along by running the water if they're having trouble going. This way will spark the necessity to pee. You are doing get to know when to prevent also. If the kid doesn't need to go, they don't need to go. You are doing not want to show potty time into game time.

Make sure you're giving your child more to drink at this point also. You would like them to possess strong body signals to find out what to do, which is simpler once they have more fluid release.

You do not want to be the sole reminder that they have to use the potty. This way will cause you to be annoying and nagging. Set a timer so that it pops, and therefore the child remembers to use the potty independently.

You will want to stay this routine in situ for several weeks to set in. simply because they need to be mastered using the restroom doesn't mean that accidents won't happen. They will. If you've got tried for several weeks and make no progress, provides it an opportunity. Stop training and check out again after a couple of months. Your child might not be ready yet.

Urinary Tract Infections

These can hinder the potty-training process. Anyone who has had a UTI knows that it's painful and uncomfortable. It also creates an urge to travel; that's not real. This fact will confuse a toddler. There are some symptoms you'll notice with a UTI like straining without urine, bad-smelling urine, color changes in the urine, many urinations with little production, etc. These infections are rare in young children, but not out of the realm of possibility.

The trouble is that when the infection is cleared up, the kid may have some bad memories, and it can take time to urge back to potty training. Twiddling my thumbs and reassuring so that they're not scared to undertake again.

When a toddler who is potty trained starts to possess many accidents, start checking for a UTI. It also can be a symbol of diabetes.

Bowel Control

Bowel control usually happens before the kid gets bladder control. There also are many signs that the kid has got to have a movement so you'll better prepare. This way usually gives you time to urge the kid to the potty before they are going.

There comes some extent where children do not have bowel movements in the dark, and it becomes a daytime-only activity. Once you notice that your child has regular bowel movements, it's appropriate to start bowel control training.

There are some distinct signs that a toddler has a movement. They'll stop playing, hide somewhere, or grunt and switch red in the face. you'll say things like, "I see you're pooping." Saying something like this helps the kid to spot what he or she is doing and, therefore, the sensations to predict once they got to attend the potty.

You want to elucidate to the kid what you're expecting and why. You would like to make sure that you explain that this often is what grownups do; this is what mommy and daddy do, and explain that since they're getting bigger, this often is what they have to do, Language like which will make it easier to convey what you're expecting to a toddler. You would like to precise it in words because children aren't ready to read your expressions and tones.

To make this easier, attempt to coordinate getting to the potty with the child's normal movement routine. If you're unsure about when this is often, take the kid to the potty about thirty minutes after a meal.

Be prepared to take a seat with your child while they are going to the potty. But if they need to be alone, that's ok also. Sometimes if there's an excessive amount of stimulation, the kid isn't ready to go, so be aware of those needs. You furthermore may want to pour on the praise when the kid does it correctly. Praise even only for attempting. You would like to strengthen that they're doing what you would like them to do.

You need to possess patience with boys also. Sometimes parents confuse learning bowel control with stubbornness in the child, which isn't always the case. Boys often devour on bladder control before bowel control. The ability to relax, constipation, or encopresis also can play an outsized role in bowel control.

Relaxation Problems

When you have a toddler that has difficulty relaxing in the restroom, there are some belongings you can do to make this process easier. The primary thing to undertake is simply sitting on the potty clothed or in a diaper. This fact will make the restroom less scary and obtain the kid comfortable with the equipment.

Once the kid is comfortable sitting in the restroom clothed, enter seated on the toilet with the edges open to use the potty but are still comfortable. Once they're comfortable with this, you'll move to lay the diaper across his or her lap then moving on to bathroom paper instead.

Constipation

Constipated children are going to be difficult when it involves potty training. If your child features a history with constipation, you'll want to attend for potty training. It's not something to stress about, just something to remember and be sensitive to when trying to potty train.

Sometimes the act of potty training is horrifying enough to cause constipation in a child. Constipation isn't merely an infrequency to supply a movement. It's predicated on the hardness of the stools produced.

For instance, if your child features a very dry movement that doesn't stick with the diaper, he or she could also be constipated. The thing to stay in mind is that simply because the action would be acceptable for an adult doesn't mean that it's for a toddler.

If you attend something like suppositories or enemas, it'll only compound the matter and make it worse. It's best to prevent potty training and check out again at a later time. Consult a doctor about why this could be occurring if the matter persists.

There are some things that you simply can do to make the painful passing of constipation on the kid. You would like to stay the kid company to make them feel safer. Lubricate the kid with petrolatum to make it easier to pass the stool. You'll also help to keep the child's cheeks apart to make it easier.

Constipation can put pressure on the bladder, which may cause accidents. This way is often indicative of needing medical attention.

If you notice a dramatic switch and find yourself seeing diarrhea, talk with a doctor as this is often a symbol of infection, allergy, etc. this will also cause potty training to be difficult as sensations aren't exact. It is often hard on the gastrointestinal system to sustain diarrhea for long periods.

There are many reasons diarrhea can occur. Consider things out of the standard like lactase deficiency or other food-related allergies. Sorbitol, the sweetening agent in sugar-free candy and gum, can cause many problems.

Encopresis

This behavior is when the kid is physically incapable of getting control over their bowels if they're over four years old. This is often not an uncommon problem to possess, affecting one to 2 percent of all children. This way is often referred to as being "fecally incontinent." This particular condition affects boys more so than girls.

Learning to use the restroom is often a stressful time for a toddler. This way suggests that the kid may suffer constipation due to this stress. Chronic constipation can cause other severe problems that make it a difficult bathroom to train a toddler. These got to be discussed with a doctor.

Hygiene

Teaching your child proper hygiene is simply as important as learning to use the potty. If the kid doesn't look out for himself or herself correctly, they will make many people very sick.

Dealing with the potty and toddlers can get quite messy. If you're employing a potty seat, you would like to require the bowl out and show the kid the right way to clean it as you'll want them to assist with this.

If there's an accident, confirm that you simply clean the kid up directly. You are doing not want the kid to urge comfortable with being dirty or which will make things much harder. When underwear is dirty, you would like to decide if you save them or trash them. Urine is relatively easy to handle, and therefore the washer will look out of that. Bowel movements will depend upon the mess made. If it's wet and mushy, it's not worthwhile. Throw the undies out.

You want to make sure that you teach the kid to wipe when using the restroom cleanly. For small girls, teach them to wipe front to back to avoid infections. She should also learn to pat, not wipe hard, to stop irritation. The kid should also wipe down the seat once they are done as germs can find themselves after that flushing.

There are some products to make this easier for the kid. Extra absorbent and potent potty tissue is suggested. Also, products like flushable wipes are great because they're durable and more thorough cleaning but sensitive enough for a child's skin.

Once finished, the kid must find out how to appropriately wash their hands. This way may reduce the spread of disease and infection. Confirm that you use warm water and antibacterial soap for fifteen seconds. You'll also sing the ABCs or count to 10 when scrubbing. This fact makes it a little more fun for the kid.

The child must dry hands on a towel that should be washed a minimum of once per week. Albeit the kid doesn't attend the potty, they ought to still wash hands. This way must be a daily practice. This way applies to you also. Confirm you're rewashing your hands.

You should remind your child to shut the lid on the restroom before flushing it. This way may reduce the spray of germs. You'll also want to show a boy that it's essential to lower the seat and lid regularly at this point again to start the habit early.

There is a simple way to make the potty seat easier to wash. You'll wrap the bowl in cling wrap or put a filter in it to make it easier to empty and clean. This way may make cleanup easier and germ transference minimal. Just confirm you are doing not flush these items; they have to travel in the trash.

You want to make sure that you simply clean a potty seat with bleach water regularly. This way could be done after every use of the potty chair, and you would like to avoid cleaning it on the carpet.

Potty-Training Techniques

The real key to success is when potty-training knows that each child is different. An equivalent potty-training method that's incredibly effective for one child might not work for an additional. This section will re-evaluate the most straightforward techniques, also as what to think about to decide if a specific system will work for bathroom training your baby.

Potty Promotion Time

If you've got a toddler who benefits significantly from routine, this is often an honest way to help them recognize their bathroom habits. It doesn't work well for youngsters who are easily frustrated or distracted but are mostly cooperative.

You will have got to choose a month that you simply can heavily specialize in potty training together with your child. Attempt to keep trips on the brink of home or to places they will use the potty. Regularly ask once they got to go and check out to assist them in recognizing what it seems like to pee and poop by getting them on the potty. This way usually leads to a minimum of partial potty training.

The disadvantage here is that an excessive amount of intensity can backfire and make potty-training harder, also because of the indisputable fact that you'll get to put aside large chunks of your time to possess a potty schedule. The advantage is that having a concentrated effort also helps your child consider learning to use the restroom.

Wait And Go

This technique is best for teenagers around age two or older, especially those that have an older sibling that they'll want to imitate. It also works well for youngsters who enjoy accomplishments and praise.

Essentially, you create potty seats accessible to your child. While you'll encourage them to travel, don't force it. Once they do pee or poop, however, give them tons of praise.

The downside of this method is that your child could also be in diapers longer, but you ought to not worry about this since Parenting Magazine reports that by the age of three, nearly 40% of youngsters are still not potty-trained. The advantage is that when your child is prepared, there'll be fewer accidents because it's what they need to do.

Rewards

Some children thrive on praise, while others need a little more to push them in the right direction. If your child is one who thrives on reward, consider offering something sort of a small sticker for going pee or an outsized sticker for doing a poop if you reward whenever though, you are doing need to take care of what your child will expect in the future.

There will come a time when your child will get to use the restroom without being compensated. Additionally, using this method sets a precedent for providing rewards for other milestones in the future. This way makes this method best for youngsters who will accept a gift like new underwear or a visit to grandma's house or the toy store, once they're using the restroom regularly.

Watching For Signs And Encouragement

Some children could also be curious about potty training but lack the knowledge of the sensations of getting to the potty. This method is best for those kids who may have to find out about getting to the potty feels before they're able to roll in the hay on their own.

Try to notice when your child pees most frequently. As a general guideline, if your child features a large drink, the kid will get to pee 45 minutes to an hour later. You ought to even be conscious of the signs that indicate your child must poop. Some hide in a corner, while others squat. You'll also notice they grunt, make a face, or that their faces turn red. Kids who need to pee may hold the world or dance around. Each kid is different, but once you recognize what yours does when it's potty time, you're one step closer to setting them on the potty while they're going.

Persistent Pottying

Your child will have a tough time having accidents if they never have an opportunity to. Start by placing your child on the potty every ten minutes. Plan your outings and trips to the shop around going somewhere that features a bathroom. Bring a potty seat to a line on the restroom, to stop your child from holding onto the edges of the larger potty, and make sure they're not scared about falling in.

This way is an excellent method for youngsters who aren't feeling the sensations of traveling to the potty. As you praise them once they produce something, they will start to relate, eliminating waste with the praise they get from using the potty.

Let Them Be Naked

Once they're beginning to use the potty and recognize the sensations, you'll allow them to be naked for periods of reception also. Just let them be naked from the waist down and keep clothes handy for when the company arrives. When your child is beginning to grasp the concept, slowly increase the problem. Add underwear first for them to figure with, then have them train with pants and underwear. Remember to avoid intricate clothing like overalls, onesies, and tight pants to assist and encourage success.

Babysitting and Traveling

Sometimes travel can't be avoided during potty training, but it's best if you'll avoid having to travel places while the kid is potty training. If you're to the purpose where the kid is usually trained, but not entirely, and it's taken longer to coach than you expected, this is often where travel tips can help.

When you leave the house, you would like the kid to be empty. This way may limit accidents. Don't provide liquids on the road and go potty before leaving. You would like to avoid putting them in training diapers because it reinforces the thought that it's okay to have an accident.

Make sure you're taking the potty seat or adapter seat with you because the child is little and can require many stops along the way. Keep an eye fixed out along the way for places to prevent so that you're ready if the kid has got to attend the potty.

Have hygiene products ready like tissues and sanitizing gels just if you can't correctly sanitize in a strange bathroom. Keeping potty tissue in the car isn't a bad idea, either. You are doing not want to possess to urge creative with a toddler.

You want to use the stall made for disabled people, so you've got many rooms, but the seat could also be above normal, so it'll require your help. Many places are now incorporating family bathrooms to make room for toddlers and fogeys, so utilize these once you can.

This way is an honest time to show more about hygiene. Have the kid place potty tissue on the seat of a weird potty. Safety is vital also so always accompany the kid to the potty. Confirm an adult is around all the time.

Make sure you've got some kind of mattress protection with you. This way will be a water-proof sheet, plastic tablecloth, bag, or bathroom mat with a rubber back. A bit like you don't want the mattress soiled reception; neither does a hotel, friends, or relatives.

It is not uncommon for accidents to occur now. If that happens, return to training pants and luxuriate in the trip. Startup again once you get home. It's an excessive amount of an exciting, stressful, fun time to urge the kid into a routine.

Be aware of the child's diet while traveling. The change in food can create a shift in movement frequency, and consistency confirms you're listening to it and react accordingly.

Understanding the Danger Involved and Taking Necessary Precautions

With everything we've come to know about potty trained, we must see the danger and disadvantages involved in the hopes of mitigating them for you so your baby can enjoy those moments not complicated you'd not be ready to handle.

It's demanding: Yes, there'll be messes, your child won't show any sign of adapting to the method in the first few weeks, you've got to pay more attention and make some sacrifices (staying tons indoors) then on. All and lots of more of this may happen, and it requires an additional effort from you to endure. That's the key, despite all the blockades on the method, there'll be a result, and it'd take longer than you'd expect.

Understand that there's an opportunity that your baby isn't physically ready for such a process: Your baby might still not be prepared for the training despite displaying all the signs for you to ascertain, your child won't be ready. This way might be from medical or directly from a toddler build up. Medically, that is, in terms of some things that aren't good with them biologically and wouldn't be noticeable at their age.

What to do in the advent of an accident: In any case, your child accidentally slips while you've got gotten hold of him or her, try not to panic, and be positive in such situations. If you any sign of distress, the kid might sense this, which might hamper their training.

Know it is about them and not you: This has to do with trying to urge the proper color, which will fit the drapes, the appropriate shape that seems pleasing enough for you. Potty training isn't about making things easy for you because the caregiver except for the kid. Therefore, anything you propose to do should reflect your child's choices. Avoid forcing them to take a seat on a potty they are doing, not like, but you fancy.

Employing a potty that their feet little the ground: you want to endeavor to get a potty that when your child sits, his or her feet small the bottom. Suppose you purchase the incorrect one, attempt to urge an ideal one. Otherwise, it'd be difficult for your child to imitate the training when it seems as if they need to fall off the potty.

Tips to Assist You as the Caregiver and the Child Throughout the Experience

Read them a book while they ease themselves, to make the experience a little brighter and somewhat enjoyable for the kid rather than viewing the training as a frightening task. Choose a book that they're conversant in. You'll equally offer them the book themselves, especially the once crammed with pictures to busy themselves with.

Even after they need to be begun to urge the hang of it, keep an eye fixed out for them. You would possibly never know once they plan to play with their poo.

Do not compare their training development with others. Every child is different and thus, adapt to things differently.

Avoid making the "I am disappointed in you" face at them. The children catch on, and it doesn't motivate them to continue. Except that even after they show they need to learn the process, they're going to mess themselves still up. Aren't getting mad; like everyone else, kids too can't be perfect all the time.

If there are any indications that your child doesn't even plan to follow your prompt, seek medical attention.

Keep an emergency kit accessible. At the start of the training, there are higher chances of accidents. Do not be alarmed; it's not as bad as you would possibly think.

Dealing with Accidents

Accidents are expected because it's uncommon that your child will grasp the concept of using the potty overnight. There are several various factors that you simply must overcome once you are potty training. Sometimes, even once you have a mixture of these things, accidents can still happen. Remember that this is often a new change for your child.

While you can't do anything, which will make sure that your child won't have any accidents, what you'll do is prepare yourself to handle them. As a parent, you'll act as a network. You want to be able to pack up after your child while not making them feel guilty or ashamed. Accidents are natural, so treat them intrinsically. Reassure your child that it's okay and help them get cleaned up as best as you'll. If an accident happens publicly, this will cause tons of embarrassment. This way often is why you want to be ready with proper supplies in the least times. During potty training, you'll get to bring a bag with you that's almost like a diaper bag. This way may act as a security net just in case an accident does happen.

Accidents that often happen reception become a learning experience. While you are doing want to assist your child get cleaned up, you'll also take the time to seek out what they felt before the accident happened. Allow them to believe the sensation of wanting to go so that they will recognize it again in the future. After explaining that this is often a traditional feeling, you'll allow your child to decorate themselves and obtainable to try again. Sometimes it does take a couple of accidents for your child to understand what feeling they ought to be expecting before using the potty.

What To Do

As soon as your child has an accident, the primary step is to urge them to feel comfortable and assured again. There's no got to delay this process because this may allow the self-doubt to start. You do not want to ruin your child's desire to use the potty again in the future, so attempt not to make accidents seem scary or bad. As you're helping your child get cleaned up, explain how accidents are normal. Allow your child to ascertain that your energy is calm, which you're not mad. Though it is often frustrating, especially once you think that potty training has already been accomplished, it's a traditional experience and an enormous part of the method.

The next step is to gauge why the accident happened. You'll ask your child about this, but an excessive amount of interrogation could end in embarrassment. Ask gently about it and why he believes that it happened. Don't be surprised if they can't offer you a particular answer; it is often confusing experience. Do your best to gauge things on your own--think about the last time your child used the potty. When the accident happened, were they doing something exciting? Did they only awaken from a nap? Keep track of the way that all of them occur to note a pattern. You would possibly be ready to prevent them from happening again in the future if you'll determine what's triggering them.

A common misconception is that accidents mean your child is regressing--this isn't always the case. Once they need the concept of potty training down, it's scarce for them to throw all of those skills away. Children are observant and great learners. It'd just take a while for them to feel comfortable utilizing these skills again. The maximum amount as you are doing not want to be too hard on your child for having an accident, you furthermore may don't want to be hard on yourself as a parent. This way is often not a sign that you have failed your child, so don't treat it intrinsically. The simplest way to handle an accident is to stay a lighthearted approach to it. From the way that you simply pack up after one to the way that you ask your child and supply words of encouragement to undertake again, this could all be done calmly and soothingly.

If you notice that accidents keep happening, consider trying to place your child in pull-ups for a brief period. This small step acts as a safeguard until you see that your child is prepared to start out wearing underwear again and using the potty. Also, this is often not a sign of regression. It merely means you want to modify your potty training to suit your child's needs. There's no telling what might trigger an accident, so it is sensible for you to supply your child with some safety and reassurance until they feel confident enough to undertake again. Don't think that you need to return to diapers; this is often taking too many steps back. Utilizing pull-ups is enough.

Make a note of any environmental changes that have occurred during the time of the accidents. These changes can make an enormous impact on your child's ability to use the potty. If you've got chosen to potty train, then switch to a daily bed in the same month, this will be an extraordinary occurrence. It might add up that your child may need some accidents in this era. Any tension in the household could also impact the frequency of accidents. If your child is witnessing tons of arguing and disagreements, this might be another trigger. Almost anything can contribute to the accidents that your child has, so confirm that you do your best to stay in a stable home environment.

Always approach your child as a sympathetic figure in their life. If anything goes on emotionally, contributing to the accidents, encourage your child to speak to you about it. Once you are open together with your child, they will be more likely to be open reciprocally. Know that posing for assistance is also okay. If the accidents continue beyond any reason that you simply can see, consulting your pediatrician is that the next step. They're going to be ready to rule out any physical ailments contributing to the accidents, like UTIs. They're going even to be prepared to assist you in asking your child to urge to the rock bottom of the rationale why the accidents keep happening.

You might notice that your child simply needs more motivation to stay using the potty. Attempt to put a rewards system in situ if you are doing not have already got one. If you do, believe in changing the frequency in which you provide rewards. An easy change like this will lead your child to feel more excited about using the potty and staying out of pull-ups. Treat your child as a private. Please do your best not to compare their reach with their friends or other children their same age. Remember, some children are naturally getting to devour on potty training faster than others.

Why They Happen

There is no concrete answer on why accidents happen, but you want to not linger over this question for too long. This way may only stress you out, leading you to pass this stressful energy along to your child. They're going to be ready to sense once you are unhappy, and that they might mistake this sense for you being disappointed with them.

Getting to the rock bottom of why accidents happen is often challenging, mainly because there are numerous factors on why they will happen. As mentioned, the environment that your child is in can play an enormous role in whether or not they need bathroom accidents.

Observe your current environment, and confirm you're taking note of anything that would appear stressful to your child. Albeit you are doing not sense it initially, your child will naturally be hyper-aware of those things. Tension is the main issue that will be felt throughout the household. Suppose there are any current disagreements or individuals at odds with each other. Do your best to figure through these for the sake of harmony. For the house environment to be as healthy and loving as possible, all members must be willing to urge along.

Ask yourself if you're giving your child enough chances to use the potty. Having proper access means your child should be ready to go whenever they feel the urge. If they're being put to bed without being given the prospect to use the potty right before, then it is sensible that accidents will begin to happen. Get into the routine of encouraging your child to use the potty right before going to bed and right after they awaken. This way also applies to naps. Whenever you're close to getting in the car to travel somewhere, encourage your child to use the potty, albeit they are doing not desire, they need to travel. Stepping into these habits at an early age means they're going to stick with your child as they get older.

You might be using the incorrect tools. If your child has outgrown the children's potty, but their only option is to use the regular potty, this will convince and be intimidating. Consider obtaining a potty seat to bridge the gap. Your child won't be ready to express this stuff to you, so you want to search for the signs on your own. Confirm that the tools you're utilizing add up to the extent that your child is at currently. An equivalent is often said for pull-ups and underwear. By observing your child's progress, you ought to be ready to determine how frequently and once they should be wearing underwear.

Sometimes, accidents will happen for seemingly no reason in the least. Potty training may be a new skill that your child is learning, and since of this, there should naturally be room for error. Your child must be ready to get the hang of tons of various things to be potty trained successfully. It's a replacement sort of skill set, which will take a while to make. While it does come naturally to some children, others have a more challenging time with it. This way often is why it's so essential that you don't compare your child to others around the same age. Progress levels will vary throughout the whole potty-training process.

When you are observant without being reactive, your child is more likely to precise any questions or concerns they need to you. Knowing that they need a secure space to debate this stuff will genuinely make a difference in their confidence level. Attempt to be there for your child the maximum amount as you'll without completely taking up. While you'll take it upon yourself to escort them to the potty every few hours and continually ask them if they have to travel, it defeats the aim of what potty training aims to offer your child--independence. They're going to got to find out how to acknowledge these cues on their own, and accidents will happen along the way. This way is often how the purpose is enforced.

Potty training becomes a life lesson in the sense that your child solely controls the action and, therefore, the outcome. With this sense of control, they're going to come to understand that they will change the result. Merely getting to the potty more frequently or having the ability to raised recognize the signs will leave fewer accidents.

Potty Training Your Child in 3 Days

A Few Days Before

Purchase your child some real underwear. You'll still want to use pull-ups in the dark for a time to make sure there are not any bedwetting accidents. However, you would like to place your child in underwear during the day. Don't use a pull-up while you're potty training. It'll only hinder the method. Putting your child in underwear will make them desire an enormous kid and make them more likely to travel potty with great care that they will keep wearing them.

You may want to do this together with your child. Letting your child detect their underwear will make them that far more excited about potty training. They will choose underwear with different colors, themes, or cartoon characters.

Purchase 3 or 4 of a budget plastic molded pots and put them around the house. One in every bathroom and one in the kitchen or space where you spend with the kid most of the time. Stick a towel below for your mobile if the child may be a kid. Speaking of youngsters, by holding your mind open, you'll cash in of nature. It takes two days to spend the summer when your child is on the brink of two and doesn't leave the house. Let your child run down naked, with an outsized tee-shirt on top to stay genitalia.

You should also prepare yourself by purchasing cleaners for your carpets and furniture. It's entirely likely that your child may have a couple of accidents in the time you're potty training. You would like to be prepared to wash it up. Get cleaners that employment on protein stains or something that's meant to require out pet stains. While keeping the cleaners out of reach of your toddler, you would like to possess them handy alongside some clean white rags so that you'll clean messes as soon as they occur to stop stains and odors.

The Night Before

As you're tucking your child specific the night, tell them that tomorrow may be a vital day. Tomorrow they're going to begin using the potty! Make it sound fun and exciting. Allow them to know that if they use the potty, they'd be rewarded. Allow them to see that they're going to tend real underwear to wear and show it to them. Albeit they helped you choose it out, remind them of it and show them again. Confirm they know that tomorrow is a crucial day and rest to make the most of it.

Arrange that no-one is home on the morning of your practice day. Please note on both the door that you simply don't need disruptions, turn your electronic device on, and shut off your mobile. For days to come, you'll give your baby all of your publicity and obey the restroom training plan guidance. Teach your kids first to inform the doll we've to travel to the potty seat. It tells her why and how to go to the potty. She should find out how to take the potty in time, take down her pants, wait for the pot to urinate, pull-up her pants, then empty the pan (with false urine), then put it back to the potty seat. The kid must also clearly complement the doll and encourage you when the toy goes to the potty chair and wees.

Give her many drinks here so she will attend the potty in abundance. Teach her how to remove her pant (it is useful to possess two sizes too big), the way to sit on her potty, and relax until she urinates or features a movement. The way to clean it, pull it up, drain the pot into the bathtub, and put it back in the potted seat.

Your child should receive awards for her correct conduct and learning. Then let the kid know what to do when she has an accident, the way to attend the restroom when she plays, get to the potty when she plays outside. She will receive rewards and praise for her dry pants, especially after being hung up in the potty for herself.

She doesn't need to wear nappies in bed that night. Leave a light-weight in the dark, and you'll place the potty seat next to her bunk. On a subsequent day, we celebrate together with her and provides her a completion certificate for bathroom training. Yes, it can happen, and in only at some point, your child is often trained in the potty!

If you've got a child, presumably, you were asked the quality question, "Is she potty trained yet?" Your reply remains more likely to be no! Ultimately it'll not be possible to find out the restroom until your child is prepared. This way usually happens when a toddler is between 18 and 24 months old. However, it's not uncommon for a toddler still to be two and a half to three years old in diapers.

Several other factors are more important than your child's age: can he stay dry a minimum of three hours a day? Could he understand simple instructions and follow them? Are you curious about "big-girls," like brushing your teeth, pack up your toys, and use your potty? If so, he could be prepared.

You need the strength, stamina, and time to participate in this critical adventure. After the initial planning and officially start this process, you've got to devote three to 5 days of intensive training to your child and his potty. After the primary learning phase, you'll need another two to 3 months of continuous effort.

We all know that it isn't easy for a parent. Crossing this developmental milestone is a superb example of how difficult it is! An experienced mommy of 4 once told me, "It's such an overrated achievement to possess a restroom trained. Sliders are very easy to wash up after accidents, reminding them to travel potty every hour and don't mention using public restrooms!

If you've got committed yourself to figure on a day-to-day basis together with your kid to master their potty learning skills, the next thing you almost certainly think is, "How am I doing potty training?" You all show signs of readiness. Enable a child to be present once you enter the potty and allow them to see movements of urine and bowels in the potty.

Permit your child to observe, little, and be familiar with the restroom.

Let your baby play potty flushing.

Read potty time books. Encourage independence: Purchase an adapter for the sunshine switch in your bathroom so your child can activate and off with none support.

Promote your child's grooming and dressing during bathroom use and your normal daily function.

Foster good hygiene and teach your child the way to clean. Buy a stool to access the restroom and sink for hand and teeth cleaning. (This may be a higher level of know-how and wishes to be monitored for a couple of years.)

IMPORTANT: if your child is uninterested or resistant - PLEASE!! Don't force the difficulty. Try again in a few weeks.

Day 1

As soon as your child gets out of bed for the day, put them in a pair of underwear. Take them immediately to the potty and allow them to attempt to go. If they don't, give them much praise and act excited about the trouble.

If your child has been on a routine schedule and typically goes to the potty at an equivalent time of the day, it'll be much easier to understand when to send them to the potty. When that time is near, be excited. Through your preparation, your child should also know what it seems like to wish to go to the potty. However, this might not be evident on a primary day. They'll be shy to go to the potty or think they will wait because they don't realize how quickly the sensation of wanting to go turns into going. However, any time your child thinks they have to go to the potty, get excited, and accompany them.

Any time your child gets on the potty but doesn't go, be positive. Help them stay excited about the prospect of using the potty. They need not lose this optimism and become frustrated. You ought to also remain calm and positive, and not get frustrated, albeit your child makes messes for you to wash up. Your child will sense your frustration, and it'll ruin the whole process.

Ask them if they know that this often is where they should go to the potty. The children are going to tell you yes, probably. Suppose they are going even a little bit more, as they could if they stopped going as soon as they realized what was happening, praise them, albeit they didn't quite make it in time. Send them off to play while you pack up the mess so that they don't realize the effort they need to cause you.

If your child goes potty on their own or together with your insistence, you ought to praise them continually and be very excited. You would possibly come up with a cheer or a song to sing whenever your child goes potty. You would perhaps even dance a little. Whatever gets them excited about the very fact that they have gone potty.

You should not give your child a treat or physical reward once they go potty. If you are doing this right off the bat, they're going to expect it still even after they ought to be potty trained. They might refuse to travel to the potty if you aren't giving them treats anymore. Giving your child treats for going potty is the same as bribing them. It's going to work for the short term, but in the future, it spells disaster.

At the top of the day, put your child in a pull-up and tell them that you simply want to make sure they sleep well so that they will roll in the hay again tomorrow. Re-evaluate the day's successes and tell them that you simply are pleased with them for his or her efforts. Allow them to know that tomorrow will be even better, and stay excited as you tuck them in.

Day 2

Once again, as soon as your child gets up, put their underwear on, and take them to the potty. Knowing that getting to, they'll be going to the potty directly; they'll hold it once they first awaken so that they will enter the potty and feel that sense of accomplishment. This way is often an excellent sign.

Today you ought to confirm that your child is pulling their underwear up and down. You ought to also teach them the way to wipe themselves with the restroom paper or flushable wipes. Allow them to attempt to become more independent today. While you ought to still suggest the potty frequently, please don't take them into the potty unless they instigate it; otherwise, you can tell that they're close to going. This way may help them associate that feeling with the necessity to go to the potty and get used to how long they need between that feeling and, therefore, the actual event.

Continue being excited for your child. Help them stay optimistic and excited about using the potty. This way may help keep them on target. It's much easier for a toddler to recollect what they're alleged to be doing and keep from getting sidetracked if they're excited about it.

Day 3

Today is that the day your child is going to be potty trained. This morning tells your child to require off their pull-up and go potty. Don't enter with them. Allow them to roll in the hay on their own. Once they have gone, they're going to be excited and run bent tell you. That's your chance to be thrilled with them.

Today your child will know once they have to go potty. They're going not to attempt to hold it but will go immediately as soon as they realize they have to travel. They're going to probably tell you something like "Hey,

Mommy! Time to travel potty!" and run into the potty expecting you to trail after. Follow your child, but don't enter the potty. Substitute the doorway and allow them to feel the independence of using the potty on their own.

Today your child will likely haven't one accident. Albeit they need one or two accidents, could you take it to beat stride? Even potty-trained children get sidetracked, engrossed live or a television program, and forget to go potty. Accidents happen. As long as there are no quite two accidents during the day, the reasons for them are obvious, don't take this as a bad sign.

By the top of the day, your child is going to be going potty sort of a pro. They're going not to need your help, and that they won't even want your help. They could tell you to travel away, that they're going potty. You should give them this independence. It will urge them to keep using the potty and take pride in their ability to do it.

By the top of today, you'll be confident that your child is out of pull-ups forever. You'll still want to use a pull-up for a few weeks in the dark until your child gets used to awakening to potty. This way will take longer than the three days to mostly potty train your child, and a few children with physical problems will need nighttime pull-ups for as long as another year.

When you and, therefore, the child was ready, it is time to start training potty. But once you begin, you cannot return. Tell your child that the painting is for babies that are no longer an infant. attend the shop and let your child select new underwear for a "big kid." Let your child throw away a couple of his old windscreens once you get home and help him placed on his underwear. There is no return. Your child will wear underwear from now on.

Don't hurry them to the pot rapidly if your kid will have an accident. You would like to warn them not to follow a crash. Try not to change them directly into dry clothes. You want to experience the uncomfortable moisture once you wet yourself. This way is often a way of coaching, which will take a couple of days. You should probably stay home for the primary few days, but I encourage you to travel on a little trip, so your child feels comfortable wearing undress. For instance, the seat straps got to be changed, and a comfort station is employed for a different experience. All place the kid in the pot every 10 minutes. Don't ASK foolish questions like "You got to go sweet potty pie!? " we're talking here to a two-year-old! Just roll in the hay because it is, don't invite permission. Don't push it, and just let him or her, whether he or she must rise immediately. Set a timeout every 10 minutes if you've got a resistant baby. It's remarkable what a child will do when the facility dynamic is withdrawn. It's time to take a seat on a pot when the "potty timer" pops.

Do not go overboard; use plaudits. Act like this often is what's expected. Be cool. You should say, "you put pee-pee in the pot as Daddy and mommy (and bigger brother and your older group of play friend... 3rd parties' gold!!) do. Don't do something from what's happening; don't waste the hours reading potty training books or children's videos. Have some" big boy shorts "or" big boy shorts "or" big boy shorts, "be beautiful again!

Asking for Help from Healthcare Professionals

Some signs to seem out for which may need medical attention are:

- A drastic change in potty habits

- An explosion or decrease in the number of loo usage times
- Runny and unformed stool
- Presence of blood in the seat and/or urine
- Cloudy urine
- Pain and extreme discomfort when your child uses the restroom

Preventing Potty Training Regression

Potty training regression is an unpleasant and painful experience for a toddler, which sneaks up quickly and quietly to children and parents-they do not know whether, when, or what caused it, and everybody reception suddenly becomes unhappy.

Families aren't pleased because the baby can't or won't use the potty. Still, the particular victim here is that the kid–his innocent brain can't work it out. Therefore, the small mind isn't adequately formed to sabotage his potty-training routine deliberately. Parents–your child doesn't plot against you!

Many things cause this, like fear, diet, environmental changes, sleep habits, unforeseen events, and public water changes. These variables should be investigated.

Fear

Don't make your kid fear potty training. Words such as: "Daddy's getting to get wild when he gets home. If you do not go potty, I'll take your favorite toy away." There are more statements, but you get the idea-don't be scared of not performing your child. For fear, your child will return to the primary potty he knew-a a diaper.

A small child who eats cereals, fruits, meat, and vegetables in a diet finds it challenging to deal with nutriment things. Excessive sweets then forth and may experience a backward pot training because the whole gastrointestinal system has typically been upgraded, and it's hard to acknowledge these foodstuffs. This way is often usually the case on trips far away from home and holiday.

Climate Change

Shopping centers, public facilities, and travel services are huge challenges for a child in potty training.

Immediately, they're in an unknown place and much far from the security and privacy of their homes.

Change in sleep habits

When the sleeping habits change, both the kid and, therefore, the parent needs to switch to a replacement potty education schedule and stay this new routine up. While a baby may sleep at a particular time, the potty practice routine must be adjusted accordingly, positively strengthened, and maintained, so that the kid learns what's expected.

Unforeseen Events

Visitors have a significant effect on a toddler. The anticipation of seeing a much-loved uncle, aunt, grandparent, a lover is all-consuming, and potty is that the last item you'll consider if you are doing. The child is concentrated on exhibiting their new toy or their current work of art on a chalkboard, and it's only too easy for folks to slide by hours, and potted learning goes unnoticed and unknown.

The tasks of caring for a toddler and a child are difficult to juggle, but parents must take time to specialize in a toddler, especially on potty training.

Change In Water System

A sudden change in the water a toddler drinks may cause constipation and discomfort. Adults will experience an equivalent disorder. I strongly encourage kids to be introduced gradually to bottled spring water a couple of weeks before an extended time far away from home. During the vacations, the baby continues to offer equivalent drinking water and gradually drives them back to the regular water system once they return home. This way may reduce the impact of the above-mentioned unfamiliar environment.

Potty training isn't a simple task for folks or children; however, liable for parenting-especially potty training-is essential. If you think that potty training is more challenging for you as a mother, you're right! This naive little child tries to find something different, foreign, awkward, and desperately tries to make sense of everything and come up with no answer. Who's got the most challenging job now?

Most parents reach some extent of disintegration, throw their arms up and walk off because it's too hard. they only shouldn't −if you let your kid run naked around the house and yard, so you do not need to bother, you're creating a monster which will take months to rectify, and therefore the boy hasn't learned.

Just because you're tired or busy, there's no excuse for neglecting the potty-training needs of your child. It is time to place your shoulder and to figure harder rather than complaining. Responsible parenting isn't natural, it's harder than any paid job you'll consider, but one factor is constant-children are children-they were always, and that they always will.

Never scold or threaten a child for not having potty training right if you would like it too - that instills fear in their minds, and actually, they're scared of getting potty.

Toddlers still eat and stick with an equal thing as they did 100 years ago. Today's little tots aren't a technology gadget; you'll escape from when you're done playing the y's small people that need parents' guidance and help in teaching them what they have to find out for all times.

Parents should confine mind they were once children and fogeys or elders had to coach them.

Potty-Related Problems and Dealing with Them

Remember that accidents do happen. Stay calm, and hold your temper. This way will be hard to do, especially once you see your carpet or floor in a mess. Take a deep breath and remember that this is often temporary. If an accident like this does happen, tell your child to vary his wet underwear and placed on a clean, dry one in a calm voice.

Once your child becomes involved in this process, he will study responsibility and realize the error he has made. Be casual about accidents, taking care not to be over-concerned. It would help if you were chary not to let them know their errors as your child will desire a failure even with a little smirk or frown. Sooner or later, he will get into the groove, unless you're always there pushing too hard.

Backsliding and Regressing

The most common issue when it involves potty training is backsliding. A blip in the otherwise smooth ride has made you think that twice about whether the child has mastered the entire process. But your child is still a kid in any case, and you can't allow stress to make you act such as you only approve of him only he's doing well. Showing that you simply are stressed reflects the strain on your child. It's counterproductive to make him feel guilty. What's the simplest way to handle this small accident?

Right after the accident occurs, clean and wash him up, and placed on a fresh set of underpants. Then, sit him on top of the potty. Make him understand that he doesn't get to go now, but you simply want him to practice sitting there. Tell him that subsequent time he wants to go, he can tell you, so that you'll assist him in going to the potty in time. Keep on telling him how much it means for him to be independent. Discuss the precise details like the sensations he gets to feel when pee or poop is coming. Keep it simple and keep it clear about the items you would like him to acknowledge and do. Pinpoint if there have been stressors that made him regress and ditch the task at hand. Did you've got to make adjustments to a replacement home, a new job, illness, or is there anything that's disrupting your daily routine as a family? If everything seems to be going well for this stuff, ask yourself if your child could start the restroom training. Did he show readiness? What were the signs? You'll get to re-do the training everywhere again once you've got located the source of the regression. If not, simply reinforcing should be ready to get you and your child back on target.

Slow Progress

Once you get into the potty-training method, you might notice specific points where your child will become delayed. This way doesn't necessarily mean that accidents are to blame; other factors can cause your child to become disinterested in being potty trained, too. One delay stems from having younger siblings. Not all children with younger siblings' experience this, but your child might begin to point out a desire to use diapers again because they miss the eye related to it.

While you'll supplement the eye as you specialize in potty training, it's natural for an older child to require to act younger to be taken care of again sort of a younger child. This way is often very usual, and it can even be seen in cases where the kid doesn't have any younger siblings. If you notice that this is often happening, you would have to enforce a far better reward system or incorporate more praise when your child uses the potty. A little bit of additional motivation will allow your child to ascertain that they're still getting attention, even after being successfully potty trained.

Boredom is another thing that will get in the way of continued success. If your child becomes tired of how you simply approach potty training, you would like to make sure that you simply are changing your methods enough to stay them interested. While books on the subject could be enough to intrigue your child initially, they could grow uninterested in these stories. You'll turn your attention to the music instead, finding interactive ways for your child to ascertain that potty training may be a great point. Small changes like these are going to be necessary along the way. Even a pair of latest underwear might be enough to urge the thrill back. As soon as you notice this boredom, you want to make a change. Staying in a rut for too long will leave your child in a place where they will start to believe that they are doing not got to be potty trained.

Aside from these delays, which will occur while you're already potty training, consider that developmental delays also can happen. These are things that you simply cannot control, and that they occur naturally, counting on your child. If your child isn't walking by the typical age, then they likely won't be potty trained by the specific period, either. Remember that this isn't necessarily a negative thing. If you push your child to start potty training too early, you're only getting to be met with frustration and disappointment. Know that it's okay to urge a delayed start because children devour on concepts very quickly. You'll be ready to move through each step faster because your child is prepared instead of struggling to accomplish the primary one. There's no right or wrong age to start potty training; only you'll decide that for your child.

Mastering the concept of potty training in the home, yet failing to do so publicly, is a different form that you simply will notice some delays. It is often difficult because your child could be great at using the restroom in the comfort of your house, but the thought of employing a comfort station can create fear or regression. Public restrooms are often very overwhelming to a toddler who is now using the toilet. Whenever possible, attempt to choose single bathrooms or family bathrooms. These are more private and typically smaller. They desire a home bathroom while still being a public option. Suppose you can't find a chance like this, attempt to bring something conversant to assist your child in entering public, and reading a potty-training book while in the restroom can remind your child that the concept remains an equivalent.

Health issues can make using the potty a painful experience. Tons of youngsters suffer from constipation, which will be challenging to travel through while learning how to use the restroom. Do your best to balance out your child's diet to stimulate a healthy gastrointestinal system. Any sort of dysfunction with their bowel movements will deter them from using the restroom. A similar case can happen if your child experiences a UTI. While none of those things are entirely preventable, you'll make sure that your child practices excellent hygiene and eats a diet to market a simple time in the restroom. Don't let the pain that comes with these health issues keep your child from eager to continue with potty training. Explaining that these symptoms are normal, which they're going to get away, will reassure your child to stay trying.

When progress is slow and erratic, you'll end up disheartened. Don't ever show your displeasure, or your child will be ready to devour on every little piece and nuance of disappointment. He might want to cooperate but is unable to regulate the workings of his body yet. Be supportive, and his motivation will soar.

Potty training time isn't time to address your child. Give reminders but don't nag. If you discover him with wet pants, encourage him rather than a stern scolding. Telling him to wash up his down accident will introduce a punitive element to the entire process of potty training. When it involves these situations, don't make your child admit that he screwed up.

Introducing Other Caregivers

Another problem that's seen in toddlers is associating the potty process with one parent. This way will cause him to refuse to use the potty unless you accompany him. Early in training, you would like to line the bottom rules. Tell him that peeing and pooping are his own "deal," which he must roll in the hay by himself, but that you only are going to be there to support him.

Because most are different, there could be a scarcity of consistency once he starts daycare or a toddler faculty. The introduction of out-of-door caregivers who might not get on an equivalent page as you're can jar the training. A number of them might not understand why it's such an enormous deal for a toddler to remain consistent in his potty-training journey. Some can overzealous in helping out. Regardless of the sort of outside caregiver you'll be handling, and it's important to bring everyone together on an equivalent page. Daycare workers may use only one approach for all the youngsters they're taking care of, and your child might not fit into that general approach. Lay out all of your must-dos for your child's individualized training. After all, you're paying good money for his or her services. You'll give out a checklist to them as guidance. You'll also inform your child what you're doing so that he will skill to cue Cousin Martha or Aunt Gina or Teacher Barbara when it's time to travel potty.

Being Busy

Kids can get very preoccupied with playing. Even after the training phase, they will sometimes encounter a snag. They'll forget or maybe refuse to require the time to travel the potty or potty once they are too engaged with fun activities. You'll help to tell him that you simply haven't seen him use the potty in a while. Let him know that he can always return to his toys once he goes to the restroom or potty.

Fending Off Night-Monsters

Once nighttime use of the potty becomes a reality, you'll want to ease any fears your child has of getting to the potty by leaving a night-light around. Make it accessible so that he can reach it if he must. This way may help dispel any nighttime fears of shadows and monsters lurking in the corners.

Dealing with a Headstrong Kid

Not all kids are alike, and once in a while, you'll draw the short straw. You'll find yourself with a child who refuses to use the potty. Regardless of how hard you are trying, you can't get him to take a seat, much less do his business in the potty or potty. Sure, the kid may be a challenge, and he features a mind of his own. But that doesn't mean you ought to hand over.

Make sure that there's nothing physical or emotional, which is causing the refusal. It might be associated with stress. If the child is in the clear, then it could boil right down to his headstrong personality. If your child's wired temperament sets him up for an argument, keep checking out management techniques that fit. Different methods exist for handling him – you only got to find them. A toddler may have tantrums due to attention-seeking behavior when his parents are too busy for him. Or it is often that a parent's irritability spills over to the kid. To line aside this level of insecurity and distrust, attempt to put aside every week of special closeness; and bonding together with your child. Do that overtime for reading, playing, talking, and cuddling. You'll then start to ascertain the defiant temperament dissolve. An angry child won't function well when trying to find out a replacement skill like potty training. You'll want to delay the potty use until she's past the troublesome issue.

Double-check your parenting reins. Sometimes, a defiant child does what he does because he feels too restricted and controlled in the other areas of his life. Handle him with the proper combination of affection and patience, and he should come around eventually.

Suppose your child is in daycare and attempt to gain insight by talking and brainstorming with her teacher. Being together with your child reception could also be different from when she's at daycare. With the assistance of the daycare caregiver, you'll both find out the simplest approach.

Remain unfazed when handling the flare-ups. Show your child that each one his tantrums are rolling off you. Keep yourself calm and don't show annoyance even once you desire to lash back at him. Promise fun times ahead and fascinate him with big-kid places and things he can do once he's potty trained. Hold on to that lure of fascination, and you'll entice him to get himself potty trained; finally, when he does choose that he's yet ready, praise him for his excellent judgment.

Training a Toddler with Disabilities

Depending on the incapacity, handling the physical aspect of a toddler with the matter varies. You'll get to provide the proper equipment for mobility, like walkers or wheelchairs. Lessen the proximity between your child and, therefore, the potty or potty. Provide safety with bars or handrails along the edges of the restroom or bathroom to cling on to. Pad the potty or seat with foam if the seat is just too hard or if it becomes too cold for him. Put waterproof sheeting on so that accidents are going to be tons easier to wash up afterward. You'll need a custom potty or chair, so source this out with the assistance of your physician. a number of the features that are modified are:

- A wheelchair with a hinged padded seat in the center will be lowered to become a commode chair.
- A manual wheelchair which will be lowered to convert into a commode to suit a typical potty
- A self-inflating cushion to help the kid with moving from his wheelchair to the restroom or potty
- Grab bars on both sides of the washroom for leverage in moving from a wheelchair or walker to the restroom.
- A padded seat ring reduces the restroom's opening to supply secure and soft seating for a too slender toddler or who needs longer potty seats.
- Potty supports with a chest strap, life belt, padded cushion, armrests, and footrests.
- Safety rails and handlebars for support, and a swing-away bar to mount by the restroom

For children with difficulty in muscle control, ask your physician when that is the best time to start training. Ask him about the body signals your child must recognize to travel to the potty. This way might vary counting on the incapacity, so an individualized approach is required. A toddler with a disability may generally have a muted sense of body, so being messy might not be as bothersome to him because it is to others.

For children with special emotional needs, like those with autism, the challenge is often mental. However, they will associate happy feelings with positive actions. Once they see mommy or daddy smiling and clapping after doing what he did, he can sense that he did something right. These actions are often demolition his clothes or flushing after he has done his business. Reinforce regeneration with every small success, because they're all important.

Tips and Tricks for Potty Training

Turn the Potty Into a Playground

Using brightly colored potty chairs and using items like books or toys can keep a toddler curious about potty training. Going overboard might not be helpful as they'll distract your child from the first task at hand, which is to use the restroom. It could also detract from a bathroom's real purpose and start viewing going potty as a sort of play.

The Feeling of Discomfort Can Help to Encourage Potty or Potty Usage

Getting wet without the helpful absorbent presence of a diaper is exceptionally uncomfortable. The avoidance of this discomfort will encourage a toddler to use the restroom.

Be the Understanding Type

Frustration is normal. To avoid taking it out on your child, remember that learning to use a potty may be a massive change for him or her. Years of employing a diaper can't be forgotten with just a snap of your fingers.

Before You Begin

Please take a while to return up with some activities which will keep your child absorbed in them, preferably things that can keep your child in an incredibly small space. They should be activities your child is up to when next going to the potty, a minimum of few days so that the kid is often comfortable leaving whatever he or she is doing to use the potty. Use the proximity to convince your child that using the potty won't distract him from the sport or activity, and he will show less resistance in leaving his training for a little time to go to the potty.

Make It Fun

You can do several things to bring some life into potty training experience. We mentioned that when your son is prepared to find out the way to pee when standing, you'll put a couple of Cheerios into the restroom water and have him aim the stream at them for exercise. This way, your son will find out how to pee inside the restroom without splashing the urine round the bathroom.

Musical Motivation

Children learn best through repetition, and a few simple songs do the trick. This way is often the rationale the alphabet and other learning materials are first taught in pieces. Because the child sings repeatedly, the knowledge in the song begins to stay in her head. Musical potties and seats are useful because once the kid releases something into the potty, the chair will start to supply a song that the kid will learn and sing with time.

Make Your Child Responsible

Although you'll be worried about whether your child can handle responsibility, especially when it involves things which will potentially be messy, be comfortable, and let your child take hold sometimes. Rather than lowering his pants for him, allow him to do himself. And rather than wiping her all the time, it will enable her to wipe herself after peeing. Instead of emptying the potty into the large potty all the time, have the kid roll in the hay for herself. Some children even begin to shut the door behind them once they enter the potty, not scared of stepping into the restroom without a parent accompanying them or needing the help of an adult. The kid starts to portray independence and authority.

Toys And Treats

Toys and treats are an essential part of potty training. In a process called conditioning, science argues that permanently behavior to stay, it must be rewarded. Exercise is employed to make a transparent distinction between a specific action and specific consequences. Taking this approach, you would like to clear an evident association between successful potty use and a gift. This way, the lesson you plan to engrain in your child will stick faster.

Toys, stickers, and other treats are samples of excellent rewards you'll use. Whenever your child uses the potty successfully, pick a present from your gift bag and hand it to him. Clapping and singing songs is additionally an honest way to appreciate the great effort. Continue the practice until the kid has found out the potty.

Minimize Stress And Mess

Whenever an accident or a series of them occur, avoid getting upset. Albeit it doesn't show on your face, your child will read it from the tone of your voice. Be of excellent cheer and trust that your child will do better next time. Involve the kid in cleaning the mess to see and learn what happens when an accident occurs.

Sometimes, accidents happen when the kid has already potty trained. Don't be discouraged. Some parents report seeing up to 3 accidents in a day, but they continue to be positive that the kid will devour from where they left. It'll be challenging to take care of your cold, but you'll see that your child will react better once you approach the difficulty with calmness. Gently remind him that he needs to aim for the potty whenever the urge comes up.

Pick The Proper Location

You do not necessarily need to put the training potty in the bathroom. If your child can't quite make it to the potty to travel potty, move the potty closer. If you discover that they're unable to seek out the potty in the dark or it takes a number of the pressure off, then leave it in their room. As your child gets better at potty training, you'll slowly start to maneuver it into the potty then move them to sit on the large potty. But this will help you avoid accidents and obtain the method down without feeling such a lot of pressure.

Don't Waste Some Time With The Pull-Ups

While there's tons of advertising that comes with using pull-ups and similar products, these can hinder your progress when it involves potty-training your baby. This way is often because the pull-ups don't feel that different from a diaper to your child. The sole difference here is that your child won't get to lie to urge them back on. Yes, they help them get the motions of putting underwear on and off down, but they're not helping with the entire idea of potty training. You'll also use a daily diaper.

If you're running into issues together with your child not catching on to training and that they are wearing pull-ups, then it's time to throw those away. If you haven't even started yet, consider skipping this step and putting regular underwear on your child instead. You'll find that it takes tons of effort out of the entire thing.

Count Down To The Last Diaper

Make an enormous deal about counting right down to the last diaper. Tell your child that when the diapers are gone, that's it and that they got to be big and go potty on the restroom (or on the training potty if you choose). This way provides them a visible of it and may help them to organize before time. You both can make a game out of counting right down to the last diaper then celebrate once they are all gone.

Do A Nightly Check

If you're handling bed-wetting on a repeat occurrence, it's an excellent time to start awakening your toddler. Do this about 1 to 2 hours after sleeping and wake them up to use the potty. You'll even keep the restroom you're training without and prepared and added in some night lights to the potty and, therefore, the bedroom so that this late-night trip is simpler.

Target Practice

This way is an excellent tool to use once you try to coach your son to travel potty while standing up. Place a couple of Cheerios or other round-shaped cereal into the restroom and let your child aim at them once they pee. Whenever the kid does it right, you'll allow them to choose a prize out of a bag of prizes. These prizes are often little trinkets from the dollar store, but it makes it more fun. Not only do they get to do a little exercise, but they also get a cool toy in the process.

With an identical idea, you'll add some coloring into the restroom bowl and allow them to see how the water changes colors once they use it. You'll even use this together with your daughter. Just have them sit on the restroom backward to make it easier to ascertain the colors change.

Learn What Their Fear Is

It is usual for a few kids to fear going on the potty, especially when it involves going number two. You'll have tried many tactics and rewards and are now frustrated that it still isn't understanding. You simply need to realize that some children feel that these bowel movements are a neighborhood of themselves and that they don't want to observe them get flushed away. You'll get to spend a while watching an anatomy book or something similar together with your child and explaining how the gastrointestinal system works. This way shows the kid that the entire process of going number two is natural and good for them to do

Go Cold Turkey

Some parents apply all the techniques in the book, but all in vain. As the child goes back to the pull-up or other similar items, they are going potty therein rather than the restroom. The best thing here is to expose the diaper and put on underwear. Go cold turkey and never look back.

This way will sometimes be messy. There'll be accidents, and it will be an excellent idea to only brace yourself for them. But going cold turkey and explaining that your child must continue the potty when it's time to go can help you urge the method done faster. It's going to be a rough few days; on the other hand, it's over, and your child is potty trained.

Use The Facility Of Imitation

Kids like to be ready to imitate the people they're on the brink of, so why not use this to your advantage. Let your son mimic dad to find out the way to potty train. Let them out on the same cloth as dad and have dad teach them the basic things they should know. They will even turn it into a game and see who can attend the potty every day. Doing this will remove the strain and be the simplest way to get your kid to start out going to the potty.

Pay Attention to the Timing

Some parents are anxious to get their child out of diapers and onto the potty that they are doing not consider whether their child is developmentally able to start potty training. Your kid must be ready before you begin on this process. No child will get to high school and still be wearing diapers. They're going to get the potty-training process down at some point, albeit it's not at an equivalent time that you simply necessarily want it.

You may find that your child learns at an impressive rate than others. Some could also be faster at potty training, while some could even be slower than yours. You'll also be ready to train your first child at 18 months, but your second needs until 24 months or more. It is essential for you to concentrate on your child and how they're developmentally doing before you begin trying to potty and train them.

Consider Letting Your Child Be Naked

Some parents find that allowing their child to be naked, or a minimum of go around without pants on made an enormous difference in how well they skilled at getting to the potty. They'll be more willing to travel without the garments on, and it's sometimes easier for you to recollect what they have to do.

Once your child has been ready to master getting to the potty without their clothes on, you'll build up to putting the garments back on and helping them use the potty. Start first with the underwear then slowly add the pants back on. It's an excellent method that works fast, and there are often no setbacks or accidents once you roll in the hay the proper way.

Use Potty Training Stickers

These can help to make potty training a little bit more fun. With these, you'll take a blank sticker and place it on the bottom of your portable potty. Then have your toddler go pee in the potty. As they are doing, the sticker will become a replacement image. Counting on the sticker you simply got, it might be a butterfly, fire engine, flower, or train.

Once the toddler is completed, you'll empty, clean, then dry the potty, and therefore the image will disappear again. These are often reusable and may last for a minimum of a couple of weeks, so you'll do a conjuring trick together with your child whenever that they use the potty.

There are tons of various ways in which you'll make potty time more fun for your baby. But with the excellent trick for your child and tons of patience, you'll be ready to get them to use the potty all on their own in no time.

Sitting Solution

Sometimes, normal is boring. It also can be difficult. Your child could also be having trouble using the potty seat or the restroom the standard way, but if you discover how around it, it'll make sitting more comfortable. For instance, if you're using the rest room seat, and your child has developed a phobia where he fears that he will slide or fall under the restroom, have him sit on the toilet backward so that he clutches on to the rear of the bathroom. Doing a poop therein position is often quite comfortable for him.

The Power of Proper Pants

Pants and underwear are a "big boy" thing, and that they demand "big boy behavior." Make your child understand that. Whenever he asks for them, remind him that big boys don't pee their pants, they pull down their underwear and conduct their business without creating a multitude. When your daughter asks to wear knickers, remind her that only big girls who don't pee or poop in their pants use them, which by extension if she is to place them on, she must behave like one among the large girls.

Speak to Your Baby

The way to get anything constructive going is through communication. No system exists without proper communication. Therefore, make sure that there's clear communication between you and your child to make potty training effectively. Think about your child's personality, likes, dislikes, and preferences in your conversations.

About Using Rewards

One of the risks of employing a reward system is creating pressure to succeed. As a result, there could also be feelings of failure or anxiety once they aren't ready to use the potty correctly or on time. Another risk is that children might expect to urge a gift or prize for doing other things like brushing their teeth, finishing their whole meal, or tidying up their toys.

Praising and Feelings of Pride

Praising a toddler for achievements can help her to feel pleased with himself or herself. This way will motivate your child to keep doing well throughout the potty-training period.

Chart Your Child's Progress Through A Visible Reminder:

Allowing your child to ascertain how far he or she has gone can encourage further efforts. A chart is often used, and a marker of some sort is placed whenever your child successfully uses the restroom. Using different features for passing urine and spending stool is often helpful also. Another suggestion would be to use unique separate charts for peeing, pooping, and staying dry throughout the night.

Other Practical Potty-Training Tips:

- Potty training during the sunny months of the year is best; you'll let your children go half-naked around the house.
- Keep your children in easily removable and washable clothes.
- Always keep a group of garments in easy reach just in case of accidents.

- Do not flush the restroom while your child is sitting thereon. The experience is often terrifying.
- Provide foods that are high in fiber to assist keep your child's stool soft.

Common Potty Mistakes to Avoid

Inconsistency

Toddlers tend to do better once they know what exactly to expect. They become more resilient and agreeable also supported how consistent you're and the way predictable the situations. The tendency of being inconsistent is you send mixed signals to your children, which might be confusing for them.

Keep regular routines and schedules. Keeping a diary and taking notes might help to stay things consistent also.

Try Not to Begin Too Soon

Regardless of whether Johnny down the road began potty preparing when he was two doesn't imply that your child will be prepared at 2. Children develop at different rates, both rationally and physically - and potty preparing is both mental and physical. Allow your child to create and develop at his speed.

Try Not to Be Negative

Positive reinforcement goes tons more remote than negative castigating. If your child has an accident, don't have a fit, or more awful, upbraid the kid for arising short. Simply utilize a "we'll improve next time" approach and confirm your child's admiration once they accomplish something right.

Try Not to Surge Preparing Your Child

Pretty much any article you see that discussions about potty preparing tips will divulge to you that you simply can't surge this stuff. Hurrying potty preparing or going at a pace that's faster than what your child is alright with is simply getting to baffle both of you and cause an excellent deal of hysteria in your child. Allow your child to steer the movement.

Try Not to Worry

When you get focused on, your child gets pushed. You don't need any anxiety or negative feelings coordinated at any part of the restroom preparing process. Try not to wrinkle your nose or negative state things. You don't need your child to attach anything negative with this experience. If you would like success in potty preparing children, remain quiet and perky.

Try Not to Be Caught Ill-Equipped

You can't close yourself and your child in your home until your child is ready to travel to the restroom, which is unreasonable - and doubtless undesirable. You ought to attend the shop, church, bent supper, and different trips to take care of a strategic distance from any issues and simply make sure you are readied. Bring wipes, a change of garments, plastic bags for ruined clothes, and possibly believe a flexible potty. Toddlers usually aren't exceptionally keen on sitting on the strange potty.

Going Overboard with Family Time

Most children value one-on-one time with their parents. This way creates deeper bonding and avoids the pitfalls of rivalry between siblings to stay your attention. Getting the family involved in potty training is okay, but an excessive amount of involvement might not be beneficial.

Try to reserve a particular amount of your time for just you and your potty-training child. This way may make him or her trust you and, therefore, the process of coaching.

Scolding and Punishment

After receiving a punishment, your child naturally becomes fearful. Whether the fear lasts for a couple of seconds or a lifetime, this is often something that impacts your child's ability to find out. When fear takes over the brain, it becomes the most focus. Albeit your child exactly knows what must be done, they could begin to second-guess themselves after being punished for not using the potty (or for having an accident). In this way, scolding or punishing your child can backfire when it involves the progress that you simply have made. It is often challenging to urge your child to an area where they do not feel this fear.

Aside from developing a fear of using the potty, punishing your child for these reasons also can strain your relationship. While punishment may be a necessary disciplinary action, sometimes they cause more damages than helping a parent when it involves potty training. Because you'll be continually allowing your child to use the potty, you would like to possess a trusting relationship in the process. Albeit the punishment isn't long-lasting, its impact could be. Children prefer to hold on to certain things that you simply won't even realize they're holding on. Alongside halting any potty-training progress, this will also cause your child to become scared of future new situations.

Overall, it is sensible to skip out on the punishment once you are potty training your child. While it is often an incredibly frustrating job for both of you, remember that every child will eventually develop the talents. It's an instinct that needs time to develop. Once you punish your child for not learning this fast enough, it causes them to feel humiliated. Imaginably, this will also impact your child's future learning abilities. They might give up if they don't get it right the time in fear of being scolded or punished.

A distressed child is one who is more likely to possess accidents. This way is often different than punishment can backfire while you're potty training. It becomes a never-ending cycle of showing your disappointment and your child feeling intimidated by it. The trick is to let your child know that potty training is feasible for all people and ages. By sending a message that it's only a "big girl" or "big boy" responsibility, this will also place the incorrect entirely pressure on them. Deduct all of the intimidating aspects that you simply can. This way may help your child feel as if they will accomplish it on their own.

By avoiding punishment, you're taking all of the strain out of the method of potty training. Many parents don't realize this until it's too late and has already tried to use punishments. A stress-free environment isn't only an excellent thing for potty training but also for the whole household. Once you are holding on to that sort of tension, it can quickly become contagious. Albeit you're trying to cover it, your child will likely sense it from you.

If you're finding it difficult to potty train without punishment, you would like to make sure that your mood and feelings are in restraint. Don't attempt to work together with your child if you're in a bad mood, no matter what causes you stress. You'll be more likely to snap or punish your child, and this is often only getting to send the incorrect messages, as you recognize. Attempt to remain in the most uplifted mood that you simply can whenever you begin potty training. The experience is meant to be fun and exciting, so you want to have a demeanor to match.

This way is when you are only getting to experience together with your child once, and it's a milestone. Regardless of what percentage ups and downs you encounter, you ought to be ready to reminisce on the experience once it's over and remember all of the positive aspects of potty training. Confirm to require breaks when necessary to stay harmony in the environment. If there's another parent in the household or somebody else who can help, attempt to alternate teaching. Having a couple of different teaching styles can help your child while also helping the parental figures stay calm and relaxed.

If you're still unsure whether or not to punish your child, remember this – a punishment should only occur when your child knowingly does something wrong. Having an accident while potty training doesn't qualify, nor does being unable to use the potty in the given moment. These are all bodily functions that your child remains trying their best to work out, so you want to do your best to support them through this process. Save the punishment for times once you enforce more respect in the parent/child relationship. When it involves potty training, your child already knows that you simply are very intimate with the subject. They're going to respect this awareness, and as they become prepared to use the potty on their own, they're going to start asking you more questions.

Denial of Drinks

Some parents believe that eliminating liquids from the child's diet in certain periods can help with potty training. Not only is this untrue, but it can make your child regress very similar to being punished does. By denying your child the request to drink something, this is often already coming from a punishment sort of approach. Because your child has done nothing wrong to deserve it, they're going to be confused and might start lashing call at the method. While it'd seem logical and helpful to chop down on the quantity of liquid that your child is drinking because you would like to help them with the accidents they're having, it just isn't a practical or long-term solution.

Nighttime is often the worst time for a newly potty-trained child. It's the time that they're going to need to hold it the longest if they're unable to urge up and use the potty on their own in the dark. Having tons to drink before bed is, of course, means that your child will need to use the potty more frequently for the next several hours. Rather than lowering on or eliminating drinks at this point, make an idea for what your child must do if they need to rise to use the potty. If your child feels prepared, this may make nighttime tons more peaceful.

Another option is to show the kid to urge out of bed and awaken a parent to assistance using the potty in the dark. Of course, this suggests that you will continually need to rise and help your child throughout the night, but it might be a fast way to teach them that they will use the potty if necessary to avoid wetting the bed. Once you prefer to accompany this method, your child will likely devour on the thought quickly. This way suggests that you should only need to remain on-call for a brief period until they feel comfortable. Confirm that the potty is well lit by nightlights, which any potty seat or other device is about up and prepared to use. It will make your child's experience one that seems more suitable to tackle alone.

We recommend using pull-ups frequently when your child must choose an extended period without using the potty. Because you don't have the option to stop when you are in the car, this will be the best thing for you to do. Your child will likely be eating and drinking in the car. And this suggests that they're highly likely to wish to use the potty. If you feel that they won't be ready to hold it during the entire duration of the car ride, then choosing pull-ups may be a smart move in this case. You want to play it by ear on what you feel your child is prepared for.

Dehydration is additionally something to concentrate on. Your child's urine is noticeably darker in color if they don't consume fluids properly. The urine becomes very yellow and may need a definite smell. Staying hydrated keeps your child's bathroom usage regular, and it allows for correct digestion. All of this will impact their overall system and skill to possess enough energy to urge through the day. If you were to deny them drinks, you'd even be sacrificing certain aspects of their health. For the likelihood to avoid a couple of accidents, it is sensible to easily hunt down another method instead of one, which will cause additional problems.

Given all of the choice options, you'll see that denying your child drinks at any given point doesn't make any sense. Potty training comes with a way of innovation-- you should be testing out new methods. Sometimes, it can take a mixture of tons of various forms. Regardless of which approach you to think about, your child will respond best to the one that permits maximum comfort and self-confidence building. Attempt to empower them as best as you can, giving them the courage necessary to feel that potty training is a task that will be mastered.

pressure To Start Out

Much like anything in life, the pressure to perform is one which will hinder progress. If you've got ever experienced excitement about something, all it takes is a push from someone with more experience to make you question your abilities. This way is often how your child feels once you push the thought of potty training. It's one thing to create excitement about the method because it's a fascinating time in any child's life, but a nagging push to start potty training won't automatically make your child want to find out. Your patience must be in check from the very beginning, even before you begin teaching.

How does one confirm that you simply aren't being too pushy, yet being informative enough to answer all of your child's questions? The simplest way to determine this is often to concentrate on how your child talks about the topic. Remember that curiosity may be a great sign! When your child is curious, this suggests that they need to think in-depth about the thought of potty training. If you notice that your child is at this stage, do your best to bring it up in conversation regularly. Explain how at some point, they're going to be using the potty too. Confirm that you simply keep each talk that you have lighthearted.

When enough curiosity is displayed, this is often generally once you will notice a number of the signs discussed that indicate your child is prepared for potty training. This way is often how the pattern forms, but know that this isn't the only way. If your child is afraid of potty training, as tons of youngsters do because they feel intimidated, confirm that you simply take this fear away as best as you'll. Show them the tools which will help them to make the experience less scary. If you pressure your child while fear is already present, this is often only getting to cause even more resistance.

No mention of potty training doesn't necessarily equate to no interest. Your child might simply grasp the concept and feel content with it, despite having no outward interest in potty training. This way is often also an excellent sign, but it is often harder to understand how your child feels once they don't express it to you. To measure your child's interest level, you'll try mentioning the subject. Again, keeping it lighthearted is usually the simplest approach. To fire up some excitement, you'll try some of the fun game ideas mentioned in the previous chapter. This way is often enough to make potty training seem attractive while also keeping the pressure minimum.

One of the worst things which will happen from pressuring your child to potty train before they're fully ready may be a regression. This way will occur at any age and any level of potty-training experience. Whether you've got been performing on it for one week or one year, an excessive amount of pressure on your child can lead them to revert to using diapers or having many accidents. This fact will be a frustrating time for you both, but it's essential to keep your child's pressure still off. If they're already feeling uncertain, a way that involves bullying won't allow them to ascertain how easy and fun potty training is. They're going to see this for themselves with the assistance of the tools and methods you simply use.

Regression is among the most fears that the parent will have when embarking on the potty-training journey. Abandoning this fear and concentrate on your child's level of progress. Because there is often no true comparison between ages and knowledge levels, you only got to work supported the knowledge that you simply see ahead of you. Sometimes, your child just won't be ready, which is okay. As mentioned, you'll simply wait a couple of more months then try again. Regression doesn't happen without reason. It's something that's triggered, whether it's situational, environmental, or personal. By remaining confident in your child, you aren't leaving any room for these regressive behaviors to make.

Many parents believe the thought of no formal potty training. This way suggests that they permit their children to become interested in using the potty whenever it happens, then they assist them in doing so when asked. There's no preparation or setup because this method revolves around the child's natural inclination to potty train themselves. This way often guarantees that you simply aren't pressuring your child to do anything that they aren't ready for. It allows them to be on top of their bodies and their life changes, an interesting approach. Regardless of what, all children will reach some extent in life where the thought of potty training becomes of interest.

Being too Helpful

Helping is okay, but to not the purpose that it creates dependency. Children, at some point, got to do things on their own. This way is often a natural progression of their development.

Instead of always offering help, try being on the sidelines and offer encouragement. Being a "cheerleader" shows reassurance that you simply are there and are supportive while allowing your child to be independent.

Conclusion

Congratulations!

You have made it to the end of *Potty Training in 3 Days*, and that I want to personally thank you for trusting us with this vital stage in your child's life.

I would like to wish you all the luck so that you're successful in potty training. You've taken the essential steps that a lot of haven't. You've taken steps to get the knowledge to recognize what you should do to achieve success.

Remember, you want to be consistent. Consistency is one of the foremost essential things that you can do immediately for your child to succeed in potty training. If there's anything you learn from us today, please let that be that consistency is crucial.

Secondly is the 'push.' Whenever your child sits on the potty, confirm they're pushing. Once they try, they will rise, albeit if they have not done anything in the restroom. It's okay for them to stand up, providing they pushed. Remember that you are responsible.

You are the parent, and you've got to line the stage. You're pulling strings, so remember that as your child is trying to push the boundaries, you've got set as a parent, and as a person's, this process may be frustrating. This process may be challenging, and we understand that; we're telling you to be parents and be human. You will be frustrated, you will be mad, and you would possibly even yell a few times.

But don't let that keep you from saying to yourself, "I'm not an honest parent." You're human, and it's getting to happen, so you've got to be yourself and do how you usually do things and be yourself and be happy and faithful to yourself. As we said, most significantly, get some rest because you do not want to be stressed in this process. You would like to possess the maximum amount of energy possible. That will not only increase the probabilities for your child's success but assist you in maintaining your sanity and improving your success also.

We wish you good luck and much fun.

Elena Gregory

Made in the USA
Coppell, TX
28 September 2021

63179620R00095